The Church in the Coming Great Tribulation

A Biblical Defense of the
Post-Tribulational Rapture and the
Second Coming of Jesus Christ

STEVE URICK

WestBow
PRESS
A DIVISION OF THOMAS NELSON

WestBow Press books may be ordered through booksellers or by contacting:

WestBow Press
A Division of Thomas Nelson
1663 Liberty Drive
Bloomington, IN 47403
www.westbowpress.com
1-(866) 928-1240

ISBN: 978-1-4497-9451-4 (sc)
ISBN: 978-1-4497-9452-1 (hc)
ISBN: 978-1-4497-9450-7 (e)

Library of Congress Control Number: 2013910738

Printed in the United States of America.

WestBow Press rev. date: 06/20/2013

Other paperbacks and eBooks by the author:

Acts One Dispensationalism
The Fundamentals of the Christian Faith
Christian Discipleship and the Local Church
Evangelism and Christian Apologetics
Practical Christian Living
Major Cults and False World Religions
False Teachings and Divisive Movements
Signs of the Second Coming of Jesus Christ
and the End of the World
Nowmillennial Dispensationalism
The Truth About Roman Catholicism

To order, go to:
www.amazon.com
www.authorhouse.com

The Church in the Coming Great Tribulation
is Part II in a prophecy trilogy.
Part I is titled: *Signs of the Second Coming of
Jesus Christ and the End of the World.*
Part III is titled: *Nowmillennial Dispensationalism: A Biblical
Examination of the Millennium and the Kingdom of God,*
a must read for Bible students interested in
the present and future kingdom of God.

This book is dedicated to all persecuted
Christians in the world, today, and in the future.

*"That no man should be moved by these afflictions:
for yourselves know that we are appointed thereunto.
For verily, when we were with you, we told you before that we
should suffer tribulation; even as it came to pass, and ye know."*

1 Thessalonians 3:3-4

Contents

Take heed that no man deceive you.

"Now we beseech you, brethren, by the coming of our
Lord Jesus Christ, and by our gathering together unto him,
that ye be not soon shaken in mind, or be troubled, neither by
spirit, nor by word, nor by letter as from us, as that the
day of Christ is at hand. Let no man deceive you by any means:
for that day shall not come, except there come a falling away
first, and that man of sin be revealed, the son of perdition."
2 Thessalonians 2:1-3

Preface

The Urgency of Our Times

Bible prophecy is a great subject. It is exciting to read and learn about what God has to say concerning the future of mankind, especially those events that surround the last days and the Second Coming of Jesus Christ. One of the most notable and blessed events in Bible prophecy is the Rapture; that is, when Christ returns to gather together all believers to be with Him, in the air, at His coming (1 Cor. 15:51-53; 1 Thess. 4:13-17). The purpose of this book is to defend what I believe is the biblical teaching of the Rapture *at* the Second Coming of Jesus Christ. I believe it is imperative in these last days that Christians seriously examine the very real possibility that we may have to go through the Great Tribulation, and so, gird ourselves spiritually in case it does happen in our lifetime.

World events are rapidly coming together, just as the ancient Hebrew prophets and the Lord Jesus predicted in the Bible. Israel, as a nation since 1948, is at the center of world attention and has become a "burdensome stone" to the nations (Zech. 12:3). The Middle East is a virtual time-bomb ready to explode into war at any time between Israel and her neighboring Arab nations (Matt. 24:6). Disputes over sovereign land rights between Israelis and so-called Palestinians, and religious tension between Jews and Muslims, have caused continual fighting and failed peace talks. Many over there are desperately searching for a solution or "peace plan" that works and will last.

The revived Roman Empire (the modern European Union) is also becoming increasingly more involved in the politics and religions of the Middle East. Recently, in April 2000, Pope John Paul II (the first pope to make an official visit to Israel) entered into Jerusalem on a peace mission, seeking to reconcile the three great monotheistic faiths of the world—Judaism, Christianity, and Islam. In August of that same year, twenty-one major religious bodies (from Orthodox and Protestant denominations) joined with the pope for ecumenical prayer at Saint Paul's Cathedral in Rome. The United Nations, the Vatican, and the World Council of Churches are all currently calling for global peace and ecumenical unity through political negotiations and interfaith "dialogue" between all the governments and religions of the world. All this points to the coming man of sin, the Roman ruler called the Antichrist and his cohort, the false prophet, who will arise on the world scene with a satanic plan to create global "peace" under a new world order and a unified false religion and/or spirituality.

Meanwhile, Christians everywhere have been bombarded in the last thirty years with many books, articles, tracts, tapes, radio and television broadcasts, the Internet, prophecy videos, CDs, DVDs, seminars, etc., by popular Christian writers and speakers, all telling us Christ can come back at "any moment" and Christians will be taken out of the world *before* the Great Tribulation occurs. (Supposedly, this doctrine was lost for almost eighteen hundred years, but has now been "recovered."). But what if they are wrong? I believe they are and many Christians will be shocked when they *face the Antichrist* on the world scene someday. This will cause much confusion and disillusionment for many people. But a sober and objective look at the scriptural possibility that the body of Christ will be present during the Great Tribulation can greatly help to mentally and spiritually prepare the last generation of Christians that must go through it in the future.

It concerns me that most churches in America do not preach or teach about a posttribulation Rapture at all (or even do a fair study of it). Few Christians are aware of the prophetic views of the early church or the development of modern dispensationalism over recent years. The modern dispensational movement, which is rooted in most fundamentalist, evangelical, and Pentecostal churches in America today, is, in reality, a recent movement that began only about 170 years ago in England, and exploded in America less than one hundred years ago (see Chapter 2). Yet most Christians have no real understanding of what dispensationalism is all about, its hermeneutic (method of interpretation), or how it has affected their beliefs.

This book looks at various misconceptions and unbalanced views that, in my opinion, modern dispensationalism promotes and examines the biblical basis for the *single* return of Jesus Christ at the end of the age and the posttribulational Rapture of the elect in Christ. But keep in mind, *only the Bible is authoritative because it alone is divinely inspired*, from cover to cover, and without error (see 2 Timothy 3:16; 2 Peter 1:20-21). Like the noble Bereans in Paul's day, we must examine any and all teachings by God's Word to determine whether or not it is true (Acts 17:10-11).

It is my prayer this book will truly edify and instruct the reader, help promote readiness for "that Day," and encourage Christian unity based on sound Bible doctrine.

1

Why Study Bible Prophecy?

Why should Christians study prophecy (future events) in the Bible? Isn't it all going to pan out in the end anyway? So what does it really matter? Besides, doesn't the subject just end up dividing Christians? Shouldn't we just concern ourselves with the more important and practical day-to-day issues of life and not be all that concerned about future events foretold in Scripture?

The Bible tells us it is necessary to have a basic understanding of the last days and Christ's return for several reasons:

1. Jesus and Paul both commanded Christians to not be deceived by any means concerning the coming of Christ and the events that lead up to our gathering together to be with Him at His return.

Jesus said, *Take heed that **no man deceive you**"* (Matt. 24:4).

Paul said, *"**I would not have you to be ignorant**, brethren"* (1 Thess. 4:13) and *"**Let no man deceive you** by any means"* (2 Thess. 2:3).

2. Many will be ignorant and deceived and led astray by false christs and false prophets in the last days.

Jesus said, *"Many shall come in my name, saying, I am Christ; and shall deceive many"* (Matt. 24:5). He also warned, that *". . . **many false prophets** shall rise, and shall **deceive many**"* (Matt. 24:11).

Is this happening today? Just look at all the false messiahs, false prophets, and dooms-day cults that have arisen in these last days, just in America alone. Joseph Smith and Brigham Young (Mormons), Jehovah's Witnesses, Mary Baker Eddy (Christian Science), Ellen G. White (Seventh-day Adventists), L. Ron Hubbard (Scientology), Charles Manson, Jim Jones, Rev. Moon (Moonies), David Koresh, Heaven's Gate, various New Age/Eastern mystic gurus, mind-science and UFO cults, and many other lesser-known false prophets and messiahs all claim to be "the way" or "a christ" in either a reincarnated form or via some other "higher conscious" state of enlightenment. All this will culminate into what the apostle Paul warned about—the coming wicked one (the Antichrist), *"whose coming is after the working of Satan, with all power and signs and lying wonders"* (2 Thess. 2:9 cf. Rev. 13).

[Note: An antichrist (Gr: *antichristos*) is not always someone who openly opposes Christ, such as an atheist or pagan, but can also be someone who appears *instead of* or *in place of* Christ, and in this sense opposes Christ. It is a counterfeit Christ. This is why many religious antichrists are so dangerous. Outwardly they profess Christ, but their teachings are false because they teach a different Jesus and a different gospel. They can be found anywhere—in churches, seminaries, colleges, universities, and in political offices. They can be pastors, popes, philosophers, professors, scientists, and statesmen. They influence many people and lead them astray. They use a continuous barrage of propaganda to deceive people and get them to believe in a lie. All this will ultimately lead to *"the* lie" which the Antichrist will use to delude the unsaved world that does not love the truth, but loves unrighteousness instead (see 2 Thess. 2:9-11; 1 Jn. 2:18, 22).]

3. The doctrine of the Second Coming of Christ is a fundamental of the Christian faith and is tied to other important doctrines as well (e.g., the Rapture, the Day of the Lord, Judgment Day).

Every Christian should become grounded in the basic doctrine of the Second Coming of Christ and the sign events that surround it. Any disagreements Christians have over this doctrine ends up dividing the body of Christ. All this is contrary to 1 Corinthians 1:10, which commands Christians to not be divided over doctrine; but rather, we should *"all speak the **same thing**, and that there be **NO DIVISIONS** among you, but that ye be perfectly joined together in the **SAME MIND** and in the **same judgment** [the same doctrinal viewpoint]."*

How do we achieve that? By avoiding the subject or accepting any and all views? No! The only way to achieve *true* unity is to carefully examine all Scriptures that are related to it. Then we can all come to the *"unity of the faith, and of the knowledge of the Son of God, unto a perfect [mature] man, unto the measure of the stature [likeness] of the fullness of Christ"* (Eph. 4:13).

4. A unified understanding of the Second Coming of Christ teaching is a powerful witness to the lost.

There are many skeptics, critics, and false religions that believe the reason Christians are divided is because we don't have the truth. How tragic! The doctrine of the Second Coming of Christ and the last days is clearly revealed in the Bible. With a little bit of study, it can easily and clearly be explained and understood, without any contradictions, by mostly any Christian, to anyone who asks.

5. Christians who are grounded in future-events teachings have greater opportunity to evangelize the lost and rescue people from cults that major on end-time teachings.

I like it when the Jehovah's Witnesses come to my door. One topic they like to bring up is the topic of future events. They are completely wrong in most of their views, but what an opportunity to witness to them and show them how they are being deceived by the Watchtower organization!

Why are not more Christians winning JWs to Christ? Is it because many Christians are not equipped to explain the fundamentals of the faith? If more Christians were grounded in the basics, it would go a long way in refuting the cults today. Instead, many Christians close the door and hide when opportunity comes knocking. Every Christian should learn how to explain their faith in *simple and concise* terms to anyone who asks (e.g., the doctrine of redemption, the deity of Christ and His bodily resurrection, the Trinity, Heaven, Hell, etc.). You do not have to know everything, but you do need to know some things.

If you are a Christian, get doctrinally grounded (if you are not yet) and be ready to offer clear truth to those caught in error. Oftentimes cultists have no answers when confronted with sound doctrine via literal interpretation (e.g., the bodily resurrection of Jesus), and will give you an ear (if you speak calmly and *gently*) as you explain key biblical truths and ask them thought-provoking questions. All this plants seeds in their minds that they can then search out later on their own. As you practice witnessing to people in all sorts of religions, and with all sorts of beliefs, you will get better and more confident over time.

[For help in getting grounded in the Bible basics and knowing what the cults teach, read the author's books: *The Fundamentals of the Christian Faith* and *Major Cults and False World Religions.* These two concise books teach the essentials and give clear answers to questions that skeptics ask most.]

6. It promotes joy and zeal for the Lord.

"Blessed [happy] is he that readeth, and they that hear the words of this prophecy, and keep those things which are written therein; for the time is at hand" (Rev. 1:3).

"And, behold, I come quickly, and my reward is with me, to give every man according as his work shall be . . .

And the Spirit and the bride say, Come. And let him that heareth say, Come. And let him that is athirst, come. And whosoever will, let him take the water of life freely" (Rev. 22:12, 17).

Jesus is the water that gives eternal life (see John 4:14). He shed His own precious blood and died on the Cross to pay for our sins and then rose bodily from the dead (1 Cor. 15:1-4). Anything that promotes knowledge and growth in the Christian experience helps keep the Christian stable and on fire for the Lord. Bible prophecy is a great enhancer to stimulate the mind. It should never be neglected by evangelists and pastors (Eph. 4:11) who have a duty to work together to instruct believers in the whole counsel of God and hold *nothing* back (Acts 20:27).

When Christians, from time to time, do a healthy study of future events in the Bible, and the blessed hope of Christ's return and the wrath to come, it will bring joy and inspire evangelistic zeal as we see the time approaching. In short, Christians will be motivated to reach out to a lost world that is in desperate need of the Savior.

[Note: There are some in heretical sects and false teachers who have made false predictions concerning the timing of the Rapture and the coming of the Lord. But that should never dissuade any Christian from studying or teaching about future events. Rather, it should spur us on to clear up any sort of confusion (the best we can), regarding what the Bible truly teaches about the issue.]

7. The study of prophecy helps to promote holiness and purity in the life of a Christian.

*"Beloved, now are we the sons of God, and it doth not yet appear what we shall be: but we know that, when he [Jesus] shall appear, we shall be like him; for we shall see him as he is. And every man that hath this hope in him **purifieth himself**, even as he is pure"* (1 Jn. 3:2-3).

Our motive for living in obedience to Christ should not be because we are afraid we will "get caught" in the act of some sin, but rather because we love God. John said that if we love God, we will keep His commandments, and His commandments are not grievous or burdensome (1 Jn. 5:2-3).

8. The study of Bible prophecy helps to protect Christians from the coming apostasy.

*"Knowing this first, that there shall come in the last days scoffers, walking after their own lusts, and saying, **Where is the promise of his coming**? For since the fathers fell asleep, all things continue as they were from the beginning of the creation"* (2 Pet. 3:3-4).

Just as in the days of Noah, there will be (and are now) mockers who doubt and completely reject what God has said will happen in the future. But the child of God who is reading his Bible, and understands the details surrounding future events, will be drawn closer to God and encouraged and strengthened to stand for the Lord as we see the day approaching, while the world is headed the opposite way to its own destruction.

9. Christian pastors and teachers who teach Bible prophecy accurately, and the various mysteries related to it, will receive a reward from God.

*"Let a man so account of us, as of the ministers of Christ, and **stewards of the mysteries** of God. Moreover **it is required in stewards, that a man be found faithful** . . . then shall every man have praise of God"* (1 Cor. 4:1-2, 5).

When Paul taught he said he "held nothing back" (see Acts 20:20-28). It is clear that Bible prophecy should be studied and taught because it is part of making disciples. The eternal destiny of souls can be greatly affected by preaching about the end-times (and many have come to know Christ as a result). It should never be thought of as being sensational or "too scary" to study or be made known.

When Christians get grounded in the basic doctrine of the Second Coming, we will see a more fervent desire to reach souls for Christ. We will also have solid hope for the future in hard times, a greater love for the Lord, and restraint on sin in the lives of true believers.

[For more information about Bible prophecy, read the author's book: *Signs of the Second Coming of Jesus Christ and the End of the World.*]

2

Dispensationalism: Yesterday and Today

Dispensationalism, i.e., the system of interpretation that recognizes differing stewardships or economies (called dispensations) in the plan of God, finds its basis in Scripture and a proper understanding of it is necessary in order to understand biblical truth. God has divided time into different eras (or ages) and has worked in various ways in human history, with various people as stewards or administrators, to accomplish His divine purpose for mankind.

For example, in Old Testament times, under the Mosaic Law in Israel, bloody animal sacrifice for atonement of sins was the only way to be forgiven of God. But in New Testament times we no longer offer animal sacrifices. Jesus was our *final sacrifice* to end all sacrifices via His shed blood on the cross, which is the basis of the New Covenant (Matt. 26:28). So every true Christian today is a dispensationalist and a covenantalist, whether they realize it or not. Just the fact that Christian churches do not do animal sacrifices today shows they all are "dispensational" and "covenantal" to a certain degree. In fact, unless one is a dispensationalist and a covenantalist, *in the biblical sense*, then that person is a either a lost person (has no faith in Christ) or they are a heretic.

When it comes to the subject of dispensationalism, a wide range of thought takes place and it can be very confusing at times. But it is really not all that difficult to sort out the truth from error if one follows basic principles of Bible interpretation and does a lot of Scripture comparison. Remember, Scripture interprets Scripture. The Bible speaks *plainly in most cases* about most subjects. Christians will find a greater degree of biblical unity today if we "test all things" and examine our views, according to the clear systematic teachings of the Bible, especially the New Testament, and not allow our own preconceived views, or traditions of men, to dictate our theology. Remember, the goal is to promote unity based on sound Bible doctrine.

The Early Church

Up until the fourth century, the early church held exclusively to a posttribulational Rapture eschatology (study of future events in the Bible); that is, Christ will return to rescue a remnant of Jews in Jerusalem and the elect saints (Christians) *after* a time of "great tribulation" upon the earth. It is interesting to read the writings of the Ante-Nicene Church Fathers (the eminent leaders of the church from the end of the apostolic age until the Council of Nicea in AD 325). Nowhere do you get the idea they were expecting Christ to return at any moment. However, they did expect the Lord to come back after the Tribulation to rescue the church from a time of intense persecution by the Antichrist:

Justin Martyr: *"The man of apostasy [the Antichrist] . . . shall venture to do unlawful deeds on the earth **against us the Christians** . . ."* Dialogue with Trypho, cx (ca. AD 135).

Irenaeus: *"And they [the 10 kings] shall . . . give their kingdom to the beast [the final Antichrist ruler] **and PUT THE CHURCH TO FLIGHT."*** Against Heresies V, 26, 1 (ca. AD 180).

Irenaeus placed the resurrection of the church (all Christian believers) after the rule of the Antichrist and in conjunction with the resurrection of the Old Testament saints (Against Heresies V, 34, 3; V; 35, 1).

Hippolytus: *"Now concerning **the tribulation of the persecution which is to FALL UPON THE CHURCH** from the adversary [the Antichrist] . . . That refers to the one thousand two hundred and three-score days [3 ½ year period, i.e., the Great Tribulation] during which the tyrant is to reign and persecute the church."* On the Antichrist, 60, 61 (ca. AD 202).

Tertullian: *"Now the privilege of this favor awaits those who shall **at the coming of the Lord** be found in the flesh [1 Thessalonians 4:15], and who shall, **owing to the oppressions of the time of the Antichrist** [i.e., the Great Tribulation], deserve by instantaneous death [Tertullian's way of saying "translation"], which is accomplished by **sudden change** [referring to the Rapture], to become qualified to **join the rising saints**; as he writes to the Thessalonians . . ."* On the Resurrection of the Flesh, XLI.

Tertullian (ca. 160-220) also identified the timing of the Rapture as being *after* the persecutions of the Antichrist during the Tribulation.

The Bible of course is the final standard for all doctrine, not church history. But it is weighty when the men who were *closest* to the apostolic era (and would have been the likeliest to know the verbal teachings of the apostles) were all literalists in their futuristic view of the coming Antichrist and *posttribulational* in their view of the Rapture. Some say the early church drifted from the original teachings of the apostles and lost the pre-trib Rapture doctrine over time. But if that were really true we could expect at least someone in the early church to have written about the pre-trib coming of Jesus Christ to rapture (snatch up) His church. But apparently no one did. The early church was unified on their understanding of the coming of the Lord and it was not the pre-trib Rapture view they held to.

[A readily available collection of writings from the early church is a 9-volume set called, *The Ante-Nicene Fathers*, ed., Alexander Roberts and James Donaldson or Google *early church writings + name of church father*.]

The Rise of Modern Dispensationalism

Dispensational theology, as many evangelical/fundamentalists understand it today (e.g., as taught in the *Scofield Study Bible*), has not always been around. In the mid-1800s, a number of "new" religious movements arose in America and England. Some of the major cults that exist today (such as Mormonism, Jehovah's Witnesses, Christian Science, and Seventh-Day Adventism) all began in the nineteenth century in America. During that same time in England, there was a great dissatisfaction with the Church of England. Many Christians were hungering and thirsting to know God's Word and had turned away from the dead formalism and ritualism of apostate Anglicanism.

At that time, a man named John Nelson Darby (1800-1882), who was ordained in the Church of England, but later separated from it, was conducting weekly Bible studies for some of these Christians who sought a more spiritual walk. They practiced the Lord's Supper every Sunday and later became known as the *Plymouth Brethren* because it was in Plymouth, England, where the tiny movement began (ca. 1831) and successfully grew under the dynamic leadership of Darby.[1]

The most significant impact this movement made was a "new" approach to the interpretation of Bible prophecy that Darby initiated, systematized, and began to popularize. Darby taught there would be a *dual* Second Coming (Gr: *parousia*) of Christ—first, "for his saints" (the Church) secretly at the Rapture, and second, the visible Second Coming "with the saints" at Armageddon, each event separated *by a seven year period.* This interpretation became the basis of the modern dispensational movement as we know it today.

[1] Darby apparently was not the first to teach a double coming of Christ at the end of the age. There is record of one Syrian church father, Ephrem of Nisibis (306-373), and a Baptist pastor, Morgan Edwards, from Philadelphia (in 1742) who espoused a two-phase coming of Christ, though it was more of a mid-trib position (see comments by Tim LaHaye in his book: *The Rapture,* Multnomah Publishers, pp. 43-44). But a pre-trib Rapture view was never taught in church history before Darby came on the scene.

The Growth of Modern Dispensationalism

Darby made seven trips to North America between 1862 and 1877, first to meet with Canadian Plymouth Brethren and then non-Plymouth Brethren evangelicals in the United States (Chicago, St. Louis, Boston, and New York), to preach, organize meetings, and gather with leaders to teach them dispensational theology. Combined with his many writings, Darby made a profound impact on American Christians and American Fundamentalism. As a result, Bible prophecy conferences were organized nationwide to promote his newly "rediscovered" form of dispensationalism that held to futurist premillennialism and the imminent (any moment) "secret rapture" of the church.

The great American evangelist of that same era—Dwight L. Moody, founder of *Moody Bible Institute* in Chicago, in 1886, was converted to dispensationalism, though, ironically, he never learned it in detail. (Moody Bible Institute remains one of the greatest Bible training schools for Christian workers, pastors, evangelists, and missionaries in the world today, and is a major center for the propagation of dispensationalism). After that, Bible prophecy conferences associated with Moody's name were all controlled by dispensationalists. Prophecy conferences also included the famous *Niagara Bible Conference*, which ran in Niagara, New York in the 1890s, to discuss and promote dispensational theology.

In 1909, the *Scofield Reference Bible* was first printed in the United States. It was a compilation of Pastor C.I. Scofield's (1843-1921) commentary notes incorporated at the bottom of the pages of a King James Bible and published by Oxford Press. More than two million copies were sold in the first generation alone. It has since been renamed *The Scofield Study Bible,* and remains a standard for dispensational interpretation to this day.

It is impossible to estimate the effect it has had in establishing Acts 2 Dispensationalism in America, but no doubt, millions of Christians have been influenced by the Scofield Bible (myself included) and have been blessed by its many insightful and practical doctrinal notes.

Dispensationalism Today

The modern dispensational movement has grown to where it now has millions of adherents and advocates, from all sorts of evangelical, fundamentalist, and Pentecostal backgrounds. There are several Bible colleges and seminaries in America that are well known for their scholarship that favor dispensational theology. *Dallas Theological Seminary* and *Moody Bible Institute* (Chicago) are two of the most well-known, *Trinity Evangelical Divinity School* in north Chicago, *The Master's Seminary* in Los Angeles (Dr. John MacArthur, president), *Bob Jones University* in South Carolina, and *Liberty University* in Virginia (Rev. Jerry Falwell, founder). Other schools that are avowedly dispensational include Grace Theological Seminary, Talbot Theological Seminary, Western Conservative

Baptist Seminary, Multnomah School of the Bible, and Philadelphia College of the Bible, and many others.[2]

Even more well-known are the many popular daily radio and TV broadcasts that promote dispensational teachings that are heard by millions all across America and around the world. Some of them include the *Through the Bible* radio broadcasts of the late J. Vernon McGee; *Grace To You* radio broadcast, Pastor John MacArthur of Grace Community Church in California; *Insight For Living* radio ministry, Pastor Chuck Swindoll (President of Dallas Theological Seminary); *Prophecy in the News* (TV broadcast out of Oklahoma); *Love Worth Finding*, Pastor Adrian Rogers (TV/radio broadcast from Tennessee); *In Touch Ministries*, Dr. Charles Stanley (TV/radio broadcast out of Atlanta, Georgia); *Zola Levitte Presents* (TV ministry from Dallas, Texas); and *Back to the Bible*, Pastor Woodrow Kroll (TV/radio broadcast from Nebraska).

Countless numbers of books have been written by many outstanding evangelists, pastors, professors, and scholars who promote modern "pre-trib" dispensationalism, such as Clarence Larkin, H.A. Ironside, Frank Gaebelein, Charles Feinberg, John R. Rice, Jack Van Impe (TV evangelist), R.B. Thieme, Lewis Sperry Chafer and John Walvoord (former Presidents of Dallas Theological Seminary), Dwight Pentecost, Hal Lindsey (notable author of *The Late Great Planet Earth*), Dave Breese, Tim LaHaye (author of the *Left Behind* series), Charles Ryrie, Dave Hunt (apologist, speaker, author), Erwin Lutzer (pastor, Moody Memorial Church in Chicago), Zola Levitte, Chuck Smith (Calvary Chapel founder, Costa Mesa, CA), William MacDonald, Charles Baker, and Cornelius Stam.

There have also been many Bible commentaries and study Bibles published that promote dispensational theology (e.g., *The Scofield Study Bible, The Ryrie Study Bible, The MacArthur Study Bible*). The Internet also is filled with articles, pro and con, about dispensationalism (Google *dispensationalism*).

[2] To date, Trinity Evangelical Divinity School is premillennial in its eschatology, but allows for various views on the Rapture to be held by its faculty and students, such as pre, mid, and posttribulationalism.

Conclusion

I have learned much from, and greatly respect, the gifted men listed above, who, though not infallible, have faithfully opened up God's Word to us down through the years. I also recommend (for the most part) that people listen to their preaching or read their writings and profit from it. Yet, I still take issue with these brethren over the form of dispensational theology they promote. I believe we are living in the last days and this is no time to be holding onto an interpretive system that is novel, highly questionable, and riddled with error.

If the majority of fundamentalist/evangelical churches in America continue to hold to classic Acts 2 Dispensationalism as their first and only choice in interpreting the Bible, and do not return to, or at least examine, the historic dispensational view that I believe the Bible truly teaches, then many Christians may end up shocked and disillusioned someday to find themselves in the Great Tribulation, wondering how they got there (after being told, over and over, that the Church would never experience it)!

The following chapters will examine the main hermeneutical (interpretation) points that divide us and defend what I believe is biblical dispensationalism vs. modern or classic dispensationalism.

[Note: I do not want the reader to think that those who hold to classic Acts 2 (Darby, Scofield, LaHaye) or mid-Acts 9 (Stam) and 13 (Baker) Dispensationalism are enemies of Jesus Christ. This would simply not be true and would be an *unfair* assessment of what I am trying to bring forth. Overall, Christian dispensationalists have been stalwart defenders of the Christian faith all along. Though there may be some errors in their dispensational and eschatological (future events) views, most of their teachings are well within biblical orthodoxy.]

3

Dispensations and the Church

One of the most controversial and misunderstood topics among believers today is the topic of dispensationalism. We have seen that dispensationalism is a system of interpreting the Bible by recognizing that God works in various ways at different times (ages) in human history. As time went along, God gave certain people a *stewardship or management* responsibility to make known His divine revelation and purpose for mankind. For example, in an Old Testament dispensation (Gr: *oikonomia*, economy, administration) God raised up Moses and gave him a message to give to the Jewish people. It was recorded in the Old Testament and was known as the Mosaic (Sinai-Torah) Law, which included the Levitical priesthood, ongoing animal sacrifices, cleansing rites (baptisms/washings), dietary laws, Sabbath-day keeping, feasts, etc. (see Leviticus, Numbers, and Deuteronomy).

In the New Testament dispensation, God accomplished salvation for mankind by sending His divine Son into the world to be our perfect and final sacrifice for sin, forever. Jesus truly is the "lamb of God who takes away the sin of the world" (Jn. 1:29). His sacrifice on Calvary ended the Old Testament dispensation of the Mosaic Law and began a new era in history—the New Covenant made by the shed blood of Jesus (read Hebrews 7-10). God later raised up Saul, who was also called Paul, to deliver the gospel (good news) of God's grace to the Gentile nations (read Acts 9, 13). We have been in the same dispensation since and will be till the day Jesus returns to inaugurate the "age to come" (Eph. 1:21 cp. Rev. 20:1-6).

The Mystery

Before we can really do a study on *eschatology* (the study of last things), we need to first look at a foundational doctrine that pertains to *ecclesiology* (the study of the church, the body of Christ) and see how this all relates to what Paul called "the mystery." How one views the mystery of the church will greatly affect how one views the Rapture of the church, its timing, and who takes part in it. In fact, it will affect how one views the entire New Testament, especially the four Gospels in relation to Paul's epistles.

The apostle Paul wrote in the epistle of Ephesians concerning the divine mystery of the church. A mystery in the Bible is something that is a secret or hidden from our understanding. A Bible mystery could also be a new revelation that was *never mentioned before* (e.g., 1 Cor. 15:51) or that there was prior veiled mention and it was *now being fully disclosed* or revealed by progressive revelations by Jesus or one of His apostles (e.g., Acts 2:25-36).

Most Christians do not realize that it is precisely here—the Ephesian mystery—where the disagreement between modern-day dispensationalism begins. Classic Acts 2 dispensationalists believe the church, the body of Christ, is *completely separate* from the Old Testament people of God (Adam, Noah, Moses, etc.). This being the supposed case, they then say Christians are "in Christ," but the Old Testament saints are not in Christ because the church began at Pentecost (Acts 2) when the disciples were baptized by the Holy Spirit for the first time (1 Cor. 12:13). Thus, we are now living in a "parenthesis" between the Acts 2 beginning of the church and the pre-trib Rapture.

Therefore, the Christians will have a *separate resurrection* from the Old Testament people of God at the end of the "mystery dispensation" of the church age. Christians will be resurrected/raptured pretribulationally (*before* the Great Tribulation) and the Old Testament saints, along with the martyred Tribulation saints, will all be resurrected separately, immediately *after* the Great Tribulation (posttribulationally).

Now this is where it all becomes crucial! If one can correctly interpret Paul's teaching concerning the Ephesian mystery, then many other pieces of the prophetic puzzle will fall into place. To misinterpret the mystery of the church, as it was revealed to the apostle Paul in Ephesians 1-3, creates a domino effect of wrong interpretations in other areas of doctrine, particularly teachings on the end-times, and specifically the Rapture and resurrection of the church.

One in Christ

Paul tells us in Ephesians 3:3, 4 that it was made known to him, by revelation, "the mystery [Gr: *musterion*] of Christ." What was that mystery? He first mentions it briefly in Ephesians 1:10:

> *"That in the dispensation [Gr: oikonomia] of the fullness of times he [God] might **gather together in ONE all things IN CHRIST**, both which **are in heaven,** and which **are on earth**; even in him."*

Paul then goes on to explain his knowledge of the mystery in more detail in Ephesians 3:6, by saying *"that the Gentiles should be **fellowheirs** and of the **SAME** [spiritual] **BODY** [of Christ], and partakers of his promise in Christ by the gospel."*

The key question to answer is this—who does this all include? Paul said in Ephesians 3:9-10 that the "fellowship of the mystery" in past ages was hidden in God, but is now made known to the church. This revealed mystery involves the whole family of God in heaven and earth (3:11, 15). Furthermore, Paul made it clear in Ephesians 2:12-16 that the Gentiles previously *". . . were without Christ, being aliens from the **commonwealth of ISRAEL,** and strangers from the [Old Testament] **covenants of promise** [made by God to the Jews], having no hope . . . But now **in Christ Jesus** ye who sometimes were far off are made nigh **by the blood of Christ**.*

*For he is our peace, **who hath made both ONE**, and hath broken down the middle wall of partition between us [the separation between Jew and Gentile]; . . . for to make in himself of twain [two] **one new man**, so making peace; And that he might reconcile **BOTH unto God** in **ONE BODY** by the **CROSS** . . ."*

What was the result of the atoning work of Christ for the Gentiles? *"Now, therefore, ye are no more strangers and foreigners, but **fellow citizens with the saints** and **of the household of God**"* (Eph. 2:19). Our citizenship in the kingdom of heaven includes all the saved of all time. The writer of Hebrews confirms this in 12:22-23—*"But ye are come unto mount Zion, and unto the city of the living God, the heavenly Jerusalem . . . to the **general assembly and church of the firstborn** [Jesus is the firstborn from the dead—see 1 Cor. 15:23], which are written **in HEAVEN**."*

Surely this must include all those who have their names written in the Lamb's book of life (Rev. 7:9-17; 20:15; 21:22-23). They are all the spiritual seed (or sons) of Abraham, *by faith,* and made part of the body of Christ (Gal. 3:6-16, 26-29; 4:26-31).

Another example of the unity of God's people of all dispensations is shown by John's description of the bride of Christ, the New Jerusalem. On the gates of the heavenly city are inscribed the names of the twelve tribes of Old Testament Israel and upon the foundations are the names of the twelve apostles, representing the New Testament Church (Rev. 21:9-12, 14 cp. Eph. 2:19-22). This means spiritual (elect) Israel and the Christian church are spiritually one in Christ. Pretrib dispensationalism keeps the Old Testament saints out of the body of Christ (or at least until the eternal state). Posttribulationalism teaches the covenant unity of all the saints of all time.

[Note: The "church" (Gr: *ekklesia*: ek = "out of," kaleo = "to call") is the people of God who have been "called out" of the world by God; thus, are the "called out ones." Every believer is a saint (Gr: *hagios*, "holy one"), from Adam to the last person saved, and is sanctified (set apart) unto God as His own possession.]

One Olive Tree and One Flock

Paul also reminds us further in Romans 11:13-25 about our covenant unity in Christ and with Old Testament Israel by illustrating the fact that we were *grafted into* the olive tree (which is Christ) by grace. The New Testament Gentiles were like a *wild* branch, whereas the Jews were *natural* branches that were cut off because of unbelief. The illustration is one tree with many branches (Jews and Gentiles from both the Old and New Testament dispensations). The only requirement to be in this spiritual tree (i.e., being in Christ) is faith in God's revealed promise of salvation at any given time in history (read Hebrews 11).

The apostle Paul calls Abraham, who was an Old Testament saint, the "father of all them that believe" (Rom. 4:11). Paul even refers to Abraham as an example of one who received imputed righteousness by faith, along with King David, who was also an Old Testament Jew (see Romans 4:2-8). This imputed righteousness places one into Christ and brings spiritual unity to the body of Christ, which is the whole family of God (Eph. 3:14-15). This applies to all those who have faith (Gal. 3:16). Therefore, in my opinion, it is wrong to think that the OT saints had "first dibs" in the spiritual plan of God, only to then be left out of being made spiritually one with, *and in*, Christ (Eph. 2:6, 12-13)!

> **"The hidden mystery plan of the ages was that God, in the fullness of time, sent forth His Son to die on the cross (Gal. 4:4-5; Eph. 2:16; 3:9), to redeem mankind and bring together ALL His elect people (the whole family of God), from all ages, both in heaven and on earth, in <u>ONE BODY</u>, under ONE spiritual Headship— Christ (Eph. 1:10, 22-23; 2:19; 3:3-6, 14-15)."**

That is why Jesus said in John 10:16 that He had other sheep (the Gentiles) which were not of this fold (the Jews) and He would bring them all together to form <u>ONE</u> FLOCK. At this point, some dispensationalists will argue that Jesus would have revealed the mystery. How could He, they ask, if it was hidden in God until Paul came along? Remember, Jesus did not reveal its *full meaning* during His earthly ministry. He began to mention it in metaphors and veiled teachings in the Gospels (cp. John 14:16-17, 23; 15:5; 17:11, 20-21), and Paul was then later given a *full* understanding or "revelation" of the mystery that Jesus began to teach beforehand.

What about Matthew 16:18?

Jesus said, *"upon this rock I WILL build my church"* (Matt. 16:18). Doesn't that prove that when Jesus spoke those words to Peter that the church, the body of Christ, *did not yet exist* and would only begin to form later, on the day *of Pentecost,* meaning Israel is not in the body of Christ? Yes and no! Peter had just confessed that Jesus is the Christ (16:16). Jesus then told him that upon this "rock" (the truth that Jesus is the Messiah) He would build His church. No one, *at that time*, was in the "body" of Christ. But that does not mean the Church (the "called-out" ones) did not exist until Pentecost or afterwards!

The Twelve apostles (minus Judas) were all Old Testament Jews before Jesus died and part of the commonwealth of Israel (and the covenant promises of God as well). But they were already "called out" and chosen by Jesus to be the foundation of the New Testament church (Eph. 2:20; Rev. 21:14), though the New Testament church age did not actually begin until the "blood of the new covenant" was shed at Calvary and the veil in the temple rent in two (Matt. 27:51). Fifty days later, at Pentecost, the inauguration (not the initial formation) of the New Testament church took place with the coming of the Holy Spirit to indwell and empower believers (Acts 2:1-4).

All dispensationalists agree that Old Testament Israel and the New Testament church are distinct from each other. The question is not whether there were two *separate* churches or people of God (that is obvious); but rather, are both the Old and New Testament saints "in Christ" today? According to the teachings of Jesus in John 10:16; 17:20-22, and Paul in Ephesians 1:10, 22, 23; 2:11-16, 19; 3:6, all the people of God, *in heaven and on earth*, are now reconciled to God as *one same body* in Christ, by the gospel.

In Colossians 1:18, 20, Paul said that Jesus *"is the **HEAD** of the **BODY, THE CHURCH**, who is the __BEGINNING__, the firstborn from the dead . . . having made peace through the **blood of his __CROSS__**, by him to reconcile **ALL things** unto himself, . . . whether they be things **in EARTH** or things **in HEAVEN**.*

All this happened before Pentecost.

In Old Testament times, most believers never received the Holy Spirit. He came upon some, but did not permanently indwell them (Judg. 14:6; Ps. 51:11). However, they did receive imputed righteousness "by faith," thus entered into covenant unity with Jehovah God who is Christ the Lord (Gen. 15:6; Rom. 4:3). In the church age, all believers are now "baptized into Christ" by the Holy Spirit via faith in Christ (1 Cor. 12:13). That is what the Ephesian mystery is all about. Regardless of how God worked in past dispensations, all believers are now in spiritual union with Christ, who is the head of the church (Eph. 1:20-23). The people of God in the Old Testament looked forward to the coming of Messiah and have been *retroactively* placed into Christ *through His death on the Cross*, along with Christians today who look back. This created one new man (Eph. 2:15-16). Thus, Calvary is the center of history, not Pentecost.

The Resurrection and the Rapture

What does all this oneness in Christ have to do with the Rapture? Lots! In order to have a rapture/resurrection of New Testament saints versus a separate resurrection of the Old Testament saints, seven years later, you must then maintain that the OT saints are not "in Christ." Why? Because Paul clearly taught—*"we [Christians] which are alive and remain unto the coming of the Lord shall not prevent them which are asleep . . . and the **dead IN CHRIST shall rise FIRST**: Then we which are alive and remain shall be **caught up** [raptured] **together** with them in the clouds, to meet the Lord in the air . . ."* (1 Thess. 4:15-17).

Everyone agrees the Old Testament saints and the Tribulation martyrs will be resurrected on the "last day." Jesus said, *"And this is the Father's will which hath sent me, that of all which he hath given me [i.e., all Christians] I should lose none, but should raise it up again at **the LAST DAY"** (Jn. 6:39 cf. 11:24; Rev. 20:4-6).

40

The last day refers to the close of the present age. The prophet Daniel also foretold there would be a resurrection of the dead after a "time of trouble" for Israel at "the time of the end" (Dan. 12:1-4). No doubt, Daniel is referring to the time of Jacob's trouble (Jer. 30:7), or the Great Tribulation period that will come upon the nation of Israel in the last days. Jesus later affirmed Daniel's prophecy in the Olivet Discourse concerning the end-times (Matt. 24:15-22).

If the Old Testament saints are "in Christ" and are raised up at the Second Coming of Christ at the end of the Great Tribulation, then the Rapture must be posttribulational, plain and simple. Thus, the whole theology of the pre-trib Rapture crashes to the ground. That is why most Acts 2 dispensationalists insist that the OT believers are not *in* Christ. But is that really sound doctrine? Not at all! The New Testament clearly reveals the Old Testament believers are "in Christ" and they were made one with Christ by His death on the Cross (Eph. 2:13-16), thus are also partakers in *all* the blessings and promised inheritances that God has to give to His covenant people (Eph. 1:3, 10-11, 18; 2:12-13).

Knowing the force of Paul's teaching concerning the unity of all the saints in Christ, some dispensationalists say the OT saints are in Christ *redemptively*, but they will not actually be incorporated into the body of Christ *until the eternal state*, when the eternal New Jerusalem city comes down out of heaven, as a bride (Rev. 21:1-14). But that is false! The Lord Jesus is spiritual Head over the church right now and reigns over ALL in heaven and on earth (Eph. 1:10, 20-23). Ephesians clearly reveals that the OT saints (or commonwealth of Israel) and the NT saints were raised up together in heavenly places, "in Christ," through the atoning death and resurrection of Jesus, and His subsequent ascension into heaven (Lk. 16:22, 26; Eph. 1:20-23; 2:6, 12-16; 4:8-10). In fact, all the saints of all ages have been "chosen in him" before the foundation of the world (Eph. 1:4).

[Note: There is absolutely no place for anti-Semitism! Jesus was Jewish and so were the apostles of the early church. Believing Gentiles have been brought into the covenant promises of God by grace through faith. In Christ, *"there is neither Jew nor Greek"* (Gal. 3:28). The death of Jesus (Y'shua), the Messiah, on the cross has made us all one "in him." There is no "one" special group of covenant people that are better than the rest. There are only the elect of God in Christ, which is the whole family of God—the spiritual body of Christ (Eph. 3:15). Paul said, *"in Adam all die, even so in Christ shall all be made alive"* (1 Cor. 15:22). So, according to Paul, one cannot be saved and not be in Christ. What about the Jews that reject Jesus today? They, like any Gentile, are lost until they submit to God and turn to Christ, by faith, by trusting in Him alone to be their risen Lord and Savior (see Acts 4:12; Rom. 10:1-4).]

The Last (Seventh) Trump

When Jesus returns there is going to be one resurrection of *all* the dead. 1 Corinthians 15:51-52 and Revelation 11:15-19 clearly teach a posttribulational resurrection and rapture of all the dead in Christ that will occur at the seventh or last trump.

> *"Behold, I show you a mystery; We shall not all sleep [die], but we shall **all** [not just some] be changed, In a moment, in the twinkling of an eye, **AT THE LAST TRUMP** [not first trump]: for the trumpet shall sound, and the dead shall be raised incorruptible, and we shall be changed [at the Rapture on the last day—Jn. 6:39-40]"* (1 Cor. 15: 51-52).
>
> *"And the **seventh angel sounded** [the last trump of Revelation]; and there were great voices in heaven, saying, 'The kingdoms of this world are become the kingdoms of our Lord [at the end of the age], and of his Christ; and he shall reign for ever and ever . . . and thy [Day of the Lord] wrath*

*is come [at the end of the Tribulation], and **the time of the
dead, that they should judged . . .**'"* (Rev. 11:15, 18).

At that time, the saints (all believers) will be judged and rewarded
by Christ (1 Cor. 3:12-15; 2 Cor. 5:10). This harmonizes perfectly
with the teachings of Paul in 1 Corinthians 15:23. Jesus is the "first
fruits" (or the first one resurrected). Then we who are His will be
raised (resurrected) or raptured (gathered together), depending if one
is alive or not "at His coming." Then comes "the end," when Jesus
delivers up the conquered kingdoms of the world to the Father, and
reigns forever (1 Cor. 15:24).

[Note: Keep in mind, in all likelihood, the seal, trumpet, and bowl
judgments in Revelation are running concurrently (or overlapping), not
consecutively. See chart on page 111.]

Dispensational Transitions

Another issue that causes dispute between pre-trib and post-trib
dispensationalists is the issue of God's dealings with Israel and the
New Testament church. Classic Acts 2 Dispensationalism says that
Israel and the church are totally separate and distinct, so in order
for God to fulfill His plan for Israel in the last days, and specifically
during the time of the Great Tribulation, the New Testament church
has to first be completely removed out of the way and taken *off the
earth* (2 Thess. 2:6-7). We will then revert back to the Old Testament
economy for seven years, i.e., the 70th Week of Daniel (Dan. 9:24-27),
while God deals with national Israel once again. But is this all truly
biblical? What saith the Scriptures?

Israel and the practice of Judaism were still in existence in the
book of Acts while New Testament Christianity was spreading all
throughout the Roman Empire. It was not until A.D. 70 that Israel

was destroyed by the Roman army, along with the Jewish Temple, forcing the outmoded animal sacrifices to finally cease. Yet God allowed one generation of Jews who practiced Judaism in Israel (see Acts 21:17-26) to co-exist with the New Testament Christian church as it continued to develop and grow. Judaism was gradually being phased out through *progressive* apostolic revelations, especially by the revelations that Paul received. Hence, it is clear from Scripture there was not a clean-cut break, but rather, a transitional overlapping of dispensations. That is *biblical* dispensationalism.

If God can work simultaneously with two separate groups at the beginning of the New Testament church age, why can't He do the same at the end of the church age? I believe that is precisely what God is going to do. During the Great Tribulation, God will work simultaneously with two groups of covenant people—Israel and the Church—to accomplish His divine plan (Rom. 11:1-27).

[Note: Judaism became obsolete when the "once-for-all" sacrifice of Christ took place at Calvary (Heb. 10:1-10). To make any blood offerings to God today is an abomination. The reinstitution of the Mosaic Law, complete with animal blood sacrifices, will make a come-back attempt by orthodox Jews in Israel during the 70th Week of Daniel (i.e., the final seven years of Israel's latter days). However, God (Jehovah) will not sanction it and will sovereignly squash the Judaistic revival by severely judging Israel's sin and by allowing the "prince that shall come" (the Antichrist ruler) to enter the rebuilt Jewish temple, in Jerusalem, in order to commit the "abomination of desolation" spoken of by Daniel the prophet, and cause the sacrifices to end (see Dan. 9:27; Matt. 24:15). Israel will then enter into a time of trouble it has never known before, nor ever shall again. It is the time known as "Jacob's trouble," the 3 ½ years of great tribulation (Jer. 30:7; Dan. 12:1; Zech. 12:2-3; 14:2; Matt. 24:22; Rev. 13:5-7). For more information, read the author's book: *Signs of the Second Coming of Jesus Christ and the End of the World.*]

Prophecy and Mystery

Modern pre-trib dispensationalism sets the church apart from Old Testament prophecy and claims the Christian church was so much of a hidden "mystery" in God that there is no prophecy in Scripture that pertains to her anywhere before Jesus taught about it in the four Gospels (Matt. 16:16; Jn. 17:20), and some even go so far as to say before Paul came along and wrote about it in Romans 16:25-26 and Ephesians 3:3-9. But, as we have seen, a divine mystery in the Bible does not necessarily mean it was not mentioned or hinted at previously. Rather, a mystery is a veiled prophecy or teaching that was later fully disclosed by further revelations by Jesus or one of the apostles.

For example, "the mystery of lawlessness," which was already working during Paul's day, pertains to the Antichrist during the future Tribulation (2 Thess. 2:7). But the Antichrist was mentioned in OT prophecy by the prophet Daniel and also by Jesus (Dan. 9:25; Matt. 24:15). Paul expounded on the mystery of lawlessness (deification of man over God) in 2 Thessalonians 2, but he obviously was not the *first* to reveal anything about the coming man of sin, the Antichrist.

Another example is what Paul called the "mystery of godliness," which refers to the incarnation and resurrection of Christ (1 Tim. 3:16). The virgin conception, atonement, and resurrection of the Messiah was prophesied in the Old Testament (Isa. 7:14; Ps. 16:8-10; 22:16), fulfilled by Jesus, recorded in the four Gospels and the book of Acts, and is more fully explained by Paul in his epistles.

Jesus said He would build His church (Matt. 16:18), but that does not mean the church (Gr: *ekklesia*) did not exist until Pentecost or until Paul got saved. On the day of Pentecost (the inauguration or "Grand Opening Day" of the NT church), 3,000 souls were ADDED to the church roster, along with the "little flock" (Luke 12:32) of 120 disciples (Acts 1:4, 15) who followed Jesus during His earthly ministry. Paul even said in Romans 16:7 that some of his kinsmen were "in Christ" *before* him. This proves the church did not begin with Paul (or sometime afterwards), nor did it start at Pentecost. The church was being formed while Christ was still on earth, starting with the Twelve (Matt. 10:1-4; Mk. 1:16-20; 3:13-19; Jn. 10:15-16; 20:18-22).

The salvation of the Gentiles on a worldwide scale was predicted in the Old Testament (Isa. 49:6 cf. Acts 13:46-47) and Jesus spoke about His church being "one flock" (Jn. 10:16), long before Paul came on the scene. Furthermore, OT prophecy supports the connection between Israel and the church in the present age. The destruction of Jerusalem (AD 70) was prophesied in the Old Testament (Dan. 9:26) and fell within the church age. The church also now occupies the time of the worldwide dispersion of Israel, predicted in Deuteronomy 28:25, 64; 30:1-4. Why can't the church co-exist with Israel during the 70th Week of Daniel? (And even if the NT church is totally separate from OT Israel, it still would not mean we *must* be raised at separate times).

In short, there is no clear biblical evidence that the church cannot, or will not, be here during the prophetic time of Daniel's 70th Week. To the contrary, the Bible indicates that the NT church will occupy on earth, till God brings the present age to a close at the end of the Great Tribulation (1 Thess. 5:1-6; 2 Thess. 1:7-10), when King Jesus comes to gather His elect (all His own) and set up His *eternal* kingdom on earth (Dan. 2:44; 7:25-27; Matt. 24:29-31; 1 Cor. 15:23-24, 52; Rev. 11:15).

Are there two Gospels?

Another area of theology that is affected by modern dispensationalism is *soteriology* (study of salvation). Classic dispensationalism teaches that the "gospel of the kingdom" (Matt. 24:14) will be preached to the whole world during the time of the Great Tribulation by 144,000 supposed Jewish evangelists (see Rev. 7:3-8; 14:1-4). While it is true that they are redeemed Jewish believers, nowhere does it say that these 144,000 "sealed servants of God" from "all the tribes of the *children of Israel*" (7:3-4) are actually evangelists who convert the nations to Christ, or that they preach a different gospel than Paul did. In short, it simply does not tell us what their exact role will be during the Tribulation, and to claim otherwise is mere speculation.

Some dispensationalists say the "kingdom gospel" is different from the "gospel of the grace of God" that Paul preached during his ministry (Acts 20:24), and that it requires water baptism for salvation. But Paul said there is only ONE gospel and any other gospel is a *false* gospel (Gal. 1:6-9). The gospel Paul preached will not be replaced with a different gospel message during the future Tribulation. The emphasis will be that the kingdom of God is at hand (near) during that terrible time, but the unchanging essential facts of the gospel will all be there.

What is the gospel Jesus and Paul preached? Jesus is the Christ, the Son of God, who came to earth, in the flesh, to save sinners by dying as a ransom for our sins on a cross, then rose bodily from the dead on the third day (Lk. 24:7, 24; Jn 1:1, 14; 3:16; 1 Cor. 15:1-4).

[Note: The "gospel of the kingdom" is the "gospel of the grace of God." Acts 20:24-25, 28:23, 31 says Paul preached "the kingdom of God" to Jews and Gentiles right up to the end of his life. Was Paul confused? No! In reality, they are simply different phrases that describe the one and only gospel of salvation. Some dispensationalists think they are "rightly dividing" the Word of God by saying there was a different "kingdom gospel" that was preached by the Twelve *to Israel*, but not by Paul to the Gentiles. But if that were true, why didn't Paul just come right out and say there was another "Jewish" gospel that saves and was different from his? Instead, he said there is NO OTHER GOSPEL than the one *true* gospel he preached and any other gospel is a *false* gospel (Gal. 1:6-7 cf. Acts 15).

The "gospel of the kingdom of God" (Mk. 1:14) initially related to the preaching of John the Baptist and Jesus to *only the Jews in Israel* (who were waiting for God's messianic-theocratic kingdom to be established on earth) and required only that a person believe Jesus is the Christ (Messiah), the Son of God, in order to be saved and have eternal life (Matt. 16:16; Jn. 3:3, 15-17; 4:25-26; 6:40); yet it was only "the beginning" or phase one of "the gospel of Jesus Christ" (Mk. 1:1, 15). After Jesus had been rejected by the nation of Israel and crucified, and then rose from the dead (phase two in the salvation plan of God), *the gospel of Christ* (Gal. 1:7), a.k.a., *the gospel of God* (Rom. 1:1) and *the gospel of peace* (Rom. 10:15), was then preached everywhere to both Jew and Gentile by all the apostles (read the book of Acts). Thus, there is only ONE GOSPEL, revealed in two phases—first, Jesus is the Christ and second, Jesus died on a cross for our sins and rose from the dead on the third day (Acts 10:36, 39-43; 1 Cor. 15:1-4).]

What about Baptism for the Remission of Sins?

In the Old Testament, under the dispensation of the law (Gal. 4:4), water baptism (washing) was a purification rite that *symbolized* cleansing of sins (Ex. 29:4; Num. 31:23-24; Heb. 6:2; 9:10). John the Baptist later came preaching a "baptism of repentance," in order to consecrate or prepare ISRAEL, *and only Israel*, for the coming Messiah and kingdom (Matt. 3:1-11). It was not a baptism for salvation, per se; but rather, baptism *symbolized* remission of sins for God's covenant people, the JEWS, after they confessed their sins and got right with God. It was sort of like a 1 John 1:9: *"if we confess our sins, he [God] is faithful and just to forgive us our sins and to cleanse us from all unrighteousness."* Christians confess their sins in order to get right with God in their personal daily walk (sanctification) with the Lord, but not to get saved.

The devout Jews that Peter preached to in Acts 2 were not a bunch of pagans who had no covenant relationship with Jehovah God. Rather, they were *devout men from every nation* who were hearing about

Messiah Jesus for the first time. When they were told that backslidden Israel was guilty of the crime of crucifying the Messiah, they were pricked in their hearts by the Holy Spirit. They then asked Peter, "What shall we do"? Peter answered, *"Repent, and **be baptized** . . . **for** [Gr: eis: because of, in order to, unto] **the remission of sins** and ye shall receive the gift of the Holy Ghost"* (Acts 2:38 cf. 22:16). This baptism was virtually identical to the baptism of repentance John preached, when the Jews came confessing their sins, with the added revelation that Jesus is the Messiah. This baptism openly marked them as *coming out of Judaism* and transitioned them into the New Testament church as disciples of Christ.

WATER BAPTISM "FOR THE REMISSION OF SINS" WAS NEVER COMMANDED OF THE GENTILES to be forgiven, or to receive the Holy Spirit. Thus, the transitional Acts 2 scenerio was unique. It cannot be repeated because there are no Old Testament Jews alive today. In short, Acts 2:38 IS NOT THE GOSPEL! It was a call for the covenant Jews to come forward publicly to accept *the* gospel message Peter preached—that Jesus is the Christ who was crucified and died for our sins, was buried, and then rose from the dead (Acts 2:21-36 cf. 1 Cor. 15:1-4). There is no other gospel!

[Note: The Twelve apostles were commissioned to preach the gospel and baptize new converts (Matt. 28:19; Acts 2:28). Paul was also commissioned to preach the gospel, but he did not emphasize baptism. He said, *"Christ sent me NOT TO BAPTIZE [in his name], but to preach the gospel"* (1 Cor. 1:17). However, many were baptized in Paul's ministry, even *after* the Jerusalem council dealt with Mosaic Law circumcision and washings (Acts 15 cf. 21:18-25), and in his 2nd and 3rd missionary journeys (Acts 18:8; 19:1-5). There is no clear command or example in Acts or Paul's letters that forbid water baptism. Paul emphasized the *priority of preaching* the gospel over water baptism. This shows water baptism was not required for salvation, nor was it necessary to receive the Holy Spirit, *at least for the Gentiles* (see Acts 10:44-48; 16:31), nor was it abolished. Christian baptism is an initiation into discipleship till Christ returns at the end of the age (Matt. 28:19-20) that outwardly proclaims one's *inward faith* and *identification with* the death, burial, and resurrection of Jesus, and new life one has in Christ (Rom. 6:3-4).

For more information regarding the meaning and purpose of water baptism during the transitional time of the early church, read the author's book: *Acts One Dispensationalism: Why the Church Existed in Acts 1 and the Answer to the Acts 2:38 Water Baptism Controversy.*]

Continuity vs. Discontinuity

It has been said the more dispensational you are, the more discontinuity (division) you see in Scripture, and the more covenantal you are, the more continuity (unity) you see in the Scripture. That is true. The key thing is to strike a *biblical* balance between the two theological camps. The Bible definitely teaches both. Each side has its strong points and weak points. It seems logical to me to abandon the tenuous weak points and hold firm to the clear strong points (but too often Christians defend theological *systems* rather than *scripture* itself).

Concerning the church, we know there is indeed discontinuity between the Old and New Testaments. But we also know, according to the Ephesian mystery, God has made us all "one in Christ" through His redemptive work on the Cross (Eph. 1-3). Continuity becomes obvious then. But dispensationalism tends to keep Old Testament Israel out of the body of Christ (they say they were not baptized by the Holy Spirit yet, thus are not part of the body of Christ). On the other hand, covenant theology tends to deny national Israel's future spiritual revival and restoration and rob her of the *future* fulfillment of the Abrahamic land covenants (Gen. 15:18; Rom. 11). In my opinion, both views are extreme and unbiblical.

Concerning salvation, most dispensationalists and covenantalists agree that salvation has always been by grace via faith in what God has revealed in each dispensation. The Law never saved anyone. It only acts as a tutor to drive us to Christ, so we can be justified by faith (Gal. 3:24). Paul clearly taught there was only one gospel in this dispensation of grace, not two (Gal. 1:6-9).

Christians are not under the Mosaic (Torah) Law because Jesus Christ fulfilled the law and died for us, thus set us free to live under grace (Rom. 3:21-31; 6:14; 7:1-4; 8:1-4; 10:4; Gal. 3-5). But Christians are not lawless. All true Christians can agree we fulfill God's law, *which is Christ's law*, when we walk in the Spirit, by faith (Jn. 15:12; 1 Cor. 9:20-21; Rom. 6-7; Gal. 5:18-26; 6:2). But we are never to revert back to law-keeping to try to be legally justified or made righteous before God (Rom. 4:16; Gal. 2-5; Heb. 7:19). Hence, there is continuity in that certain *moral-ethical laws* are reiterated in the New Testament and discontinuity because the shed blood and atoning death of Christ has made Old Testament Judaism obsolete. Christians do not sacrifice animals, observe Jewish holy days, Sabbaths, circumcision and purifications (washings), nor have to abstain from unclean (non-kosher) foods (Acts 10:11-16; 15:1-29; Gal. 2:11-14; Col. 2:16).

Concerning the kingdom of God, we know Christ brought a spiritual kingdom to mankind (Matt. 12:28) and He is reigning right now in heaven (Ps. 2:1-12; 1 Cor. 15:24-25; Eph. 1:20-22; 2:6). In the future, the Lord Jesus Christ will return to set up a kingdom *on earth* that will never pass away (Dan. 2:44; 7:9-27; Rev. 11:15). Thus, there is continuity between the *present* spiritual kingdom of God on earth and in heaven (Matt. 6:10), and discontinuity because a future kingdom is *yet to come* on earth, along with the New Jerusalem city (Matt. 25:34; Rev. 21-22).

[Note: Covenant theology views the Christian church as *spiritual* Israel (Rom. 9-11; Gal. 3:26-29; 6:16). However, many covenantalists *ignore or reject* God's irrevocable covenant promise to restore Israel to her land, now (even though Israel exists today) and in the future (Gen. 13:14-15; 15:18; Ezek. 37-39)! Covenant theology replaces physical circumcision (which was done on male infants in Old Testament Judaism) with *infant* water baptism (for salvation or entrance into grace), thus perverts the real meaning and purpose of *believer's* baptism for born again disciples of Christ and places one under a false Judaized form of Christianity. Paul warned the Galatians about those who would come and *pervert the gospel of Christ* and try to put Christians under legalistic bondage to false traditions of men and ritualistic practices to obtain salvation or spirituality (Gal. 3-5; Col. 2). Christians need to know what biblical covenantalism and true dispensationalism is in order to be scripturally balanced and to be able to identify and avoid any unbiblical teachings covenant theology and modern dispensationalism might promote. For more information about covenant theology, read the author's book: *False Teachings and Divisive Movements*.]

Conclusion

If one believes Paul was given a totally new and separate "mystery" *program* (instead of just a *revelation* of the mystery) for the dispensation of the New Testament church, and that it was great enough to merit a separate coming of Christ to rapture the church pretribulationally (or midtribulationally for that matter), then how can any pre or mid-trib, Acts 2 dispensationalist be sure that the Matthew 28:19-20 commission Jesus gave pertains to the Christian church today? The church will supposedly not even be here to fulfill it, since Matthew 28:19-20 goes to the end of the age, at the visible Second Coming of Christ!

Paul was not given a different commission than the other apostles for the "body of Christ" (though he was the apostle sent *to the Gentiles*). Rather, he was given new revelations that expounded upon what Jesus *began to teach* in the Gospels, concerning various "mysteries of the [present] kingdom," the unity of the "one flock" in Christ (Jn. 10:16) and the massive growth of the church after the ascension of Christ *to the end of the age*, when Jesus comes with His angels to harvest the world (see Matthew 13:36-43).

Not only did Paul expound on the meaning of the mystery of the unity of the church (Eph. 1-3), but he also gave further details about the mystery of our "gathering together" (the Rapture) of the saints in the future (1 Thess. 4:16-17). These mysteries do not strip Israel, the wife of Jehovah (Gal. 3:7-29; Eph. 2:12-14) of her covenant blessings *in Christ*, as traditional or classic (Acts 2) Dispensationalism tends to do (e.g., such as taking away Old Testament Israel's covenant unity *with* the New Testament saints, *in* the body of Christ, and *as* part of the spiritual bride of Christ—Rev. 21:9-14).

None of the mysteries in the Bible prove that the present church on earth is absolutely distinct and *totally separate* from the rest of God's people from other dispensations. In fact, the opposite is true! Jerusalem is the mother of *all* the heirs of salvation, Abraham's seed (Gal. 3:29; 4:26). Neither do any of the practices or teachings of Jesus in the Gospels, or in the transitional time of Acts, merit or prove that a brand new mystery dispensation began when Paul got converted to Christ in Acts 9, or anytime afterwards, as some ultra-dispensationalists (e.g., O'Hair, Baker, Stam, Bullinger) have claimed (though they did get it partly right concerning the purpose of water baptism for the remission of sins *for the Jews* in Acts 2). Baptists, Catholics, Lutherans, Churches of Christ, and Apostolic Pentecostals need to learn more about this.

The Twelve apostles practiced water baptism. So did Paul. There is no solid biblical proof that water baptism was a transitional Jewish practice that was to end a few years later in the Christian church age. The kingdom gospel Jesus taught in John 3:3, 16, and explained to His disciples in Luke 24:7, 27, is the *beginning* (Mk. 1:1) of the *same* grace gospel Paul ultimately preached to all in 1 Corinthians 15:3-4 and Acts 20:24-25. The mystery of the spiritual oneness or unity of all believers *in Christ* that Jesus began to teach about, *in veiled form*, in John 10:16 ("one flock") and 17:21 ("one in us"), was later fully explained by Paul in Ephesians 1-3.

Keep in mind, the mystery centers *on Christ*, not the church. He is the center of history. His work on the Cross provides salvation for the church and unity in the body of Christ through His shed blood. There were transitional changes that took place from the OT dispensation into the NT church age during early years of the first century Christian church, when new revelations were forth-coming and Israel was being set aside because of her unbelief and rejection of Jesus (Yeshua), the Messiah (and God foreknew what Israel would do). But with the atoning "it is finished" death of Christ at Calvary, the New Covenant (Testament) church age officially began, not sometime afterwards (cp. Matt. 27:51; Jn. 19:30; 1 Cor. 11:25; Heb. 9:14-16). (See appendix chart: "A Dispensational Overview of Four Ages"). We have been in that same dispensation since and will remain there until the visible, physical, Second Coming of Christ, when the Lord Jesus returns to set up His kingdom on earth and inaugurate the "age to come" (cp. Matt. 24:3; 28:20; Acts 1:11; Heb. 9:28).

Biblical "post-trib" dispensationalism upholds normal, literal, and grammatical principles of interpretation. It sees the continuity and co-equal unity of all the saints of all time; thus, correctly interprets the mystery plan of God for the church, the body of Christ. Classic Acts 2 and Mid-Acts dispensationalism does not; thus, in my opinion, should be abandoned.

The Mystery, the Body of Christ
OT Saints (before Israel) + true Israel + the NT Church = The Whole Family of God
(Ephesians 1:10; 2:14, 16, 19; 3:6, 15)

The New Covenant was made with Israel only (Jer. 31:31-34), but the Gentiles have become beneficiaries through faith in Christ.

Old Testament Believers	New Testament Believers
From Adam to the thief on the Cross who turned to Jesus.	From the thief on the Cross to the last person saved at the return of Christ at the end of the age.
In the Lord (Jehovah/Jesus) by faith in the gospel promise of the coming Messiah.	"In Christ" by faith in the gospel of Jesus.
OT saints were retroactively placed into Christ via the blood sacrifice of the Cross.	All believers (Jew and Gentile) are made partakers of the New Covenant by faith in the blood of Christ.
Jews were natural branches of the spiritual olive tree (Christ) by faith in the promises of God.	Gentiles today are grafted into the olive tree as wild branches in Christ.

One Flock (Jn. 10:16)
One in Christ (Eph. 2:13-14)
One New Man (Eph. 2:15)
One Body (Eph. 2:16; 4:4, 6)
One Spiritual Loaf (1 Cor. 10:17)
One Olive Tree (Rom. 11:16-26)
One Bride of Christ (Rev. 21:9-14)
One Future Coming of Christ
(Matt. 24:29-31; Heb. 9:28; 1 Cor. 15:23-24)

4

Imminency and the Day of the Lord

One of the most important pillars of the pre-trib Rapture is the doctrine of the imminent return of Christ. Imminency is defined by pretribulationalists to mean that Jesus Christ can come back at "any moment." Thus, there are no prophecies to fulfill or signs required in order for Jesus to come back secretly, to snatch the Christians away and take them back to heaven. After that, all the signs of the Tribulation that Jesus predicted in Matthew 24 would come to pass, leading up to the visible Second Coming of Christ to planet Earth.

Matthew 24 describes the "signs of the times," or the events that Jesus said must take place before His coming (Gr: *parousia*) at end of the age. Most pretribulationists disregard the Olivet Discourse by Jesus as having anything to do with the Rapture because they say it was a mystery, not revealed until years later by Paul (1 Cor. 15:51-53). They go on to say the Christian church will be "caught up to meet the Lord in the air" sometime *prior* to the revealing of the Antichrist and the Great Tribulation. Thus, the gathering together of "his elect from the four winds" at the end of the tribulation (Matt. 24:31) refers to the remaining dispersed Jews from around the world who will be brought back into Israel by angels, just prior to the millennial kingdom.

But is that what Jesus and Paul really taught? And are there no signs required before the "day of Christ" happens, when Jesus comes back to gather together those who are His at the Rapture? What saith the Scriptures?

Paul wrote two letters, I and II Thessalonians, that dealt with end-times. A simple comparison of Scripture with Scripture should answer this crucial question—Is the Rapture a signless event that can happen at any moment? To find out, we need to examine what Paul had to say about the Rapture in his two letters to the Thessalonians.

2 Thessalonians 2:1-3 and 1 Thessalonians 4:15-17

*"Now we beseech you, brethren, by **the coming of our Lord Jesus Christ**, and by **our gathering together** [the Rapture] **unto him**, that ye be not soon shaken in mind, or be troubled [nervously anxious], neither by spirit, nor by word, nor by letter as from us, as that **the day of Christ** [i.e., the day of the Lord] **is at hand** [near, imminent, impending, about to happen].*

*Let no man deceive you by any means: for **that day** [of the Rapture] **shall not come**, except there **come a falling away** [religious defection, rebellion, or apostasy] **first**, and that **man of sin** [the Antichrist] **be revealed**, the son of perdition"* (2 Thess. 2:1-3).

The Thessalonian Christians had been experiencing persecution and suffering for their faith in Christ. To make matters worse, a false teacher-prophet apparently sent word to the struggling believers telling them that the "day of Christ" (i.e., the Rapture) was "at hand" (near or imminent). As a result, the news made them confused and very distressed because they thought they might be entering, or had entered into, the time of the Great Tribulation that was predicted by Jesus.

It was classic end-times hysteria, much like we see in our modern times. Someone starts a rumor that the end of the world is "near," or the Rapture is about to happen, and gullible people who don't know their Bibles get all upset and quit their jobs, and sell their homes and go hide in the woods, or tell all their family, friends and neighbors that the Tribulation is upon us and/or Jesus is about to return at any moment (see 2 Thessalonians 3:6-14 warning about living disorderly as a result).

Paul wrote the Thessalonians to calm them down and straighten them out concerning the whole confusing mess. He reminded them that the "day of Christ" (the Rapture) cannot occur "except there come a falling away first" (the worldwide apostasy or religious defection from Christianity and rebellion against God, led by the Antichrist and the false prophet, see 2 Thess. 2:4-12; 1 Jn. 2:18; Rev. 13) and *"that man of sin [the Antichrist] be revealed."* Since those two things did not happen yet they (the Thessalonians) were not, and could not be, in the Tribulation, and the Rapture was certainly not "at hand" or about to happen!

Many pretribulationalists say the Thessalonians received bogus information from a false teacher-prophet, telling them they *missed the Rapture* (or possibly that *the resurrection was already past*—see 2 Tim. 2:18) and they were in the Tribulation, which they say is part of the Day of the Lord. But how could the believers miss the "Day of Christ" (the Rapture) if it had come? The Rapture is for believers! They certainly did not believe in a partial rapture theory (a false doctrine promoted by some in our *modern times* which claims that only *some* "worthy" Christians will go up in the Rapture), especially when the entire Christian church (including Paul) was still on earth during their time.

Paul clearly informed the Thessalonians in his first letter that the Rapture is for *all* Christians and they would all be gathered together to meet the Lord in the air when He comes.

*"For this we say unto you by the word of the Lord, that we which are alive and remain unto the **coming** [parousia] of the Lord shall not prevent them which are asleep [those that have died].*

*For the Lord himself shall descend from heaven with a shout, and the voice of the archangel, **and with the trump of God**: and **the dead in Christ shall rise first: Then we which are alive and remain shall be caught up together with them in the clouds to meet the Lord in the air:** and so shall we ever be with the Lord"* (1 Thess. 4:15-17).

It seems to me that any letter to the contrary would have been disregarded as being erroneous just as fast as if someone got on the radio or wrote a book or letter today, telling Christians that the Rapture had come and we all missed it! It would be laughable and ludicrous! Paul was not given a brand new rapture teaching by God that was completely unrelated to the end-time teachings of Jesus. The Christians, especially Paul, were familiar with Old Testament predictions of calamity and our Lord's teaching in Matthew 24. They knew before Jesus would return, there would be a time of great tribulation that would come upon the whole world, and Jesus would "gather together" His elect at the very end (Matt. 24:31).

The details of this "gathering" were a veiled mystery, until Paul unveiled it in 1 Thessalonians 4:15-17. Paul was reminding the Thessalonians that the Day of Christ (or Day of the Lord) will not occur until *after* the Antichrist is clearly revealed, plain and simple. When the Christians SEE the Antichrist then, *and only then*, can they become concerned about the fact that the Great Tribulation has come, or is about to happen, and the Second Coming of Christ is near.

Paul even said in 2 Thessalonians 1:5-10 that the troubled Christians would not receive justice or deliverance or rest from their trials and sufferings until *". . . the Lord Jesus Christ shall be **revealed***

*[Gr: apokalypsis] from heaven **with his mighty angels, in flaming fire** taking **vengeance** [Day of the Lord's wrath] on them that know not God, and that obey not the gospel of our Lord Jesus Christ: Who shall be punished with everlasting destruction from the presence of the Lord, and from the glory of his power; **when he shall come to be glorified** in his saints, and to be admired in all them that believe . . . in **that day** [the Day of the Lord/Christ/Almighty God]."*

Paul obviously was referring to the posttribulational Second Coming of Christ. Christians will experience suffering and tribulation right up to the end of the age, when Jesus comes back in flaming fire, with His mighty angels, to gather us together to be with Him. Paul's teaching completely agrees with Jesus' teaching in Matthew 24:29-31, which says, *"Immediately **AFTER the tribulation** of those days . . . then shall appear the [cosmic] sign of the Son of man in heaven . . . , And he shall send his **angels with a great sound of a trumpet** [1 Thess. 4:16] and they shall **gather together his elect** [1 Thess. 4:17] from the four winds, from one end of heaven to the other."*

The Day of the Lord

Another issue that divides pre and posttribulationalists is the issue of "the Day of the Lord" and "the Day of Christ." The Day of the Lord is the time mentioned in the Old and New Testaments when God will bring terrifying divine judgment upon the earth in a way never known before. The Day of Christ is "that day" when Christ comes back to gather together (rapture) all those who are His (2 Thess. 2:2).

Posttribulationalists say the Day of the Lord is the Day of Christ (Christ is Lord) and it comes immediately *after* the Great Tribulation. Some pretribulationalists believe the Day of the Lord is the Day of Christ, but that it comes *before* the Tribulation. Other pretribulationalists say the Day of the Lord/Christ never refers to the

Rapture, but only to the day of God's wrath at the end of the Great Tribulation. Other pre-tribbers say the Day of the Lord is not the Day of Christ (the Rapture); thus, by making a distinction between the two phrases, they divide the coming of Christ into separate events, seven years apart—the Rapture and the revelation.

So who is right? What saith the Scriptures?

Isaiah 2:12, 17, 19:

*"For **the day of the Lord** of hosts shall be upon every one that is proud and lofty, and upon every one that is lifted up; and he shall be brought low . . .*

*And the loftiness of man shall be bowed down, and the haughtiness of men shall be made low: and the Lord alone shall be exalted in **that day** . . . And they shall **go into the holes of the rocks, and into the caves of the earth**, for fear of the [returning] Lord, and for the glory of his majesty, when he ariseth and shake terribly the earth."*

This day is the day of God's wrath when the Lord Jesus Christ comes back to judge and make war against His proud enemies (see Revelation 6:15-17; 19:11-19).

Isaiah 13:6, 9, 10, 11a:

*"Howl ye; for **the day of the Lord** is at hand; it shall come as a destruction from the Almighty . . . Behold the day of the Lord cometh, cruel both with **WRATH** and fierce anger, to lay the land desolate: and he shall destroy the sinners thereof out of it.*

*For the **stars of heaven** and the constellations thereof shall NOT GIVE THEIR LIGHT: the **SUN SHALL BE DARKENED** in his going forth, and **the MOON SHALL NOT CAUSE HER LIGHT TO SHINE** [cosmic disturbance and signs in the heavens]. And I will punish the world for their evil, and the wicked for their iniquity . . .".*

Joel 2:1b, 2:

*". . . for the **day of the Lord** cometh, for it is nigh [near] at hand; A day of <u>darkness</u> and of gloominess, a day of clouds and of thick darkness [cosmic disturbance] . . . there hath not been ever the like, neither shall be any more after it, even to the years of many generations."*

Joel 2:30-31:

*"And I will show **wonders in the heavens** and in the earth, blood, and fire, and pillars of smoke. The SUN shall be turned into <u>darkness</u>, and the MOON into blood [cosmic signs in the heavens], <u>BEFORE</u> the great and terrible DAY OF THE LORD"* (cf. Matt. 24:29; Rev. 6:12-13).

The cosmic signs in the heavens happen right *after* the Tribulation and are the key events that precede the Day of the Lord.

Amos 5:18-20:

*"Woe unto you that desire the day of the Lord! To what end is it for you? **The day of the Lord is <u>darkness</u>**, and **not light** . . . Shall not the day of the Lord be darkness, and not light? Even very dark, and no brightness in it?"*

Most premillennialists say the Day of the Lord includes the Millennium. But is the Millennium dark and gloomy? Furthermore, if the 70th Week of Daniel is the Day of the Lord (as many Acts 2 dispensationalists claim), is that also an entire time of darkness and gloominess? Obviously the Day of the Lord is a single day *at the end* of the Tribulation, when Christ literally returns in judgment.

Zephaniah 1:14-18:

*"The great **day of the Lord** is near, it is near, . . . even the voice of the day of the Lord: the mighty man shall cry there bitterly. That day is a **DAY OF WRATH**, a day of **trouble** and **distress**, a day of wasteness*

and desolation**, a day of <u>DARKNESS</u> and <u>GLOOMINESS</u>, a day of clouds and THICK DARKNESS.** *A day of the trumpet and alarm against the fenced cities . . .*

And I will bring distress upon man, that they shall walk like blind men, because they have sinned against the Lord: and their blood shall be poured out as dust, and their flesh as the dung. Neither their silver nor their gold shall be able to deliver them in the **day of the Lord's wrath***; but the whole land shall be devoured by the* **FIRE** *of his jealousy . . .".*

Zechariah 14:1-4, 6-7:

"Behold, **the day of the Lord cometh***, and thy spoil shall be divided in the midst of thee. For I will gather all nations against Jerusalem to battle [Armageddon], and the city shall be taken, and the houses rifled, and the women ravished; and half of the city shall go forth into captivity, and the residue of the people shall not be cut off from the city. Then shall the Lord go forth, and fight against those nations, as when he fought in the* **day of battle***.*

And **his feet shall stand in that day upon the Mount of Olives** *[at the Second Coming of Christ], which is before* **Jerusalem** *on the east . . . And it shall come to pass in* **that day***, that* **the light shall not be clear, nor dark** *[cosmic signs in the heavens]:*

But it shall be **<u>ONE DAY</u>** *which shall be known to the Lord, not day, nor night: but it shall come to pass, that at* **evening time** *it shall be light . . .".*

Zechariah describes the Day of the Lord as "the day" the Lord actually returns to Jerusalem. It is in no way a seven-year period of time (Daniel's 70th Week); but rather, it shall come on ONE solar day and the Lord will return in the evening (Jerusalem time).

Matthew 24:29-30:

*"**Immediately <u>AFTER THE TRIBULATION</u>** of those days shall the SUN be DARKENED, and the MOON shall not give her light,*

*and the **stars shall fall** from heaven, and the powers of the heavens shall be shaken [the Day of the Lord cosmic signs in the heavens]:*

*And then shall appear the sign of the Son of man in heaven: and then shall all the tribes of the earth mourn, and **they shall <u>SEE</u> THE SON OF MAN COMING** in the clouds of heaven with power and great glory."*

The Day of the Lord cosmic signs mentioned in the Old Testament are reiterated by Jesus in the Olivet Discourse. It is obvious that Jesus placed the Day of the Lord immediately *after* the Great Tribulation.

Revelation 6:12-17:

*"And I beheld when he had opened the sixth seal, and, lo, there was a great earthquake, and **the SUN became BLACK AS SACKCLOTH of hair,** and the **MOON BECAME AS BLOOD;** and the **stars of heaven** [meteorites] **fell unto the earth** [the Day of the Lord cosmic signs] . . . and the heaven departed as a scroll when it is rolled together; and every mountain and island were moved out of their places.*

*And the kings of the earth, and the great men, and the rich men, and the chief captains, and the mighty men, and every bondman, and every free man, **hid themselves** in the dens and in the rocks of the mountains; And said to the mountains and the rocks, Fall on us, and **hide us from the face of him** that sitteth **on the throne** [the revealing of Christ at His visible Second Coming to judge], and from the [Day of the Lord] wrath of the Lamb; For the **great DAY of his WRATH is come**; and who shall be able to stand?"* (cf. Isa. 2:12, 19).

The sixth seal of Revelation, chapter 6, takes us to the time of the Day of the Lord and the visible Second Coming of Christ, after the first five seals are opened. The first five seals reveal the entire Great Tribulation period in a brief overview.

The key to understanding the book of Revelation is to know that it does not run consecutively in its chronological order; but rather, it is a concurrent layout of visions that overlap and give new prophetic details in each successive chapter, like an onion being pealed, layer by layer, or like transparency layouts of the anatomy of a man in a biology book—first the skeleton, then organs and muscles, and then the skin.

Revelation 19:11, 15:

*"And I saw heaven opened, and behold a white horse; and he that sat upon him was called Faithful and True [King Jesus], and in righteousness he doth judge and make war . . . And out of his mouth goeth a sharp sword, that with it he should **smite the nations**: and he shall rule them with a ROD OF IRON: and he treadeth the winepress of the fierceness and **wrath** of Almighty God [the Day of the Lord's wrath]."*

It is absolutely clear from the Word of God that the Day of the Lord is a "day" that is brief, cataclysmic, and utterly horrible. It is "the day of vengeance" when God Almighty (the Lord Jesus Christ) comes back to earth, in power and great glory, to make war and utterly and completely destroy all His enemies (Rev. 19). It is a unique day of judgment, completely separate, and unlike all others.

[Note: Jesus (Hebrew: *Yeshua*; Greek: *Iesous*) is Jehovah (Lord) God in the flesh, the Alpha and the Omega, and second member of the triune Godhead (the Trinity)—John 1:1, 3, 14; Rev. 1:8, 11, 13-18; 2:8; 22:12-13. Remember, the Bible says there is only one true God (1 Tim. 2:5). The only way to make sense out of the Bible is to accept the revelation that God (Elohim) is a triune Being: Father, Son, and Holy Spirit. For more information, read the author's book: *The Fundamentals of the Christian Faith.*]

As a Thief in the Night

Having established the biblical fact that the Day of the Lord is a unique, single "day" of divine wrath that comes immediately *after* the Great

Tribulation, we can now look at the Day of the Lord in relation to Christ coming as "a thief in the night." The phrase, "a thief in the night," was used by Jesus, Paul, Peter, and John to describe the sudden and unexpected coming (parousia) of the Lord. Many pretribulationalists say this phrase refers to the Rapture. However, it does not so much refer to the Rapture (even though the Rapture does occur at that time); but rather, to the return of Christ in the future to bring judgment upon unsuspecting *unbelievers* on the Day of the Lord.

As we shall see in the following verses, Christ will indeed come back as a thief in the night. But it will not be at the start of the 70th Week of Daniel (pretribulationally), nor will it happen at the mid-point of Daniel's 70th Week, just prior to the start of the Great Tribulation (midtribulationally). The thief will come posttribulationally, immediately prior to the Day of the Lord, to bring wrath and judgment.

Matthew 24:43-44:

*"But know this, that if the goodman of the house had known in what watch **THE THIEF** would come, he would have **WATCHED**, and would not have SUFFERED his house to be broken up.*

*Therefore **BE YE ALSO READY**: for in such an hour **as ye think not** the Son of man cometh."*

It has been said by some pretribulationalist teachers that this is one of the strongest verses in the Bible that favors a pre-trib Rapture. They say with all the destruction going on during the 3 ½ years (or 42 months) of Great Tribulation (Rev. 11:3; 12:6; 13:5), how could any *Christian* not think Jesus was going to come soon? But that misses the point of the passage. The Lord is not describing the Rapture in this verse, per se, and even if He was it would still be posttribulational because the context is all about the Second Coming of Christ.

Jesus is giving a warning to those who live carelessly and without any concern for the coming judgment of God. Their house will be "broken up" and they will suffer great loss, just like the people of Noah's day that were taken away in the flood and perished or like the hypocrites (or false brethren in churches) who are warned about God's coming judgment but do not prepare for it (Matt. 24:37-51).

1 Thessalonians 5:1-6:

*"But of the times and seasons, brethren, ye have no need that I write unto you. For yourselves know perfectly that the **DAY OF THE LORD** so cometh **AS A THIEF** in the night.*

*For when they shall say, Peace and safety; then **sudden destruction cometh upon them** [unbelievers], as travail upon a woman with child; and they shall not escape.*

*But ye, brethren [Christians], are not in darkness, that **that day** [of the Lord] should overtake you **as a thief** [unawares, by surprise] ... Therefore let us not sleep, as do others; but **let us WATCH** [for the warning signs that indicate the return of the Lord is near] and be sober."*

It has been widely taught by pretribulationalists that Jesus comes back "as a thief" to the Christians. But again, that misses the main point of what Jesus and Paul were really teaching! Jesus comes back "as a thief," not to the watching Christian, per se, but to an unsuspecting world of unbelievers (including many in Israel) and careless hypocrites (tares) in the churches to bring vengeance and wrath upon them *"in that day"* (2 Thess. 1:7-10).

Christians (as well as Israel) are to WATCH for the key travailing SIGNS of Christ's return (such as the Antichrist and the Great Tribulation), and so, be spiritually awake and ready to meet Him when He does suddenly return. Like birth pangs, when the signs begin to take place, and increase in intensity, then Christians can "lift up their heads" for our redemption is drawing near (imminent). All this means Christians should have an *expectant* attitude toward the Lord's return as we wait and watch for our Blessed Hope from heaven (Tit. 2:13). When the signs come to pass then, *and only then*, will the coming of Christ be imminent or impending. Only those who do not heed the warning signs will be caught by surprise (1 Thess. 5:4).

2 Peter 3:10, 12:

*"But the **DAY OF THE LORD** will come **AS A THIEF** IN THE NIGHT; in the which the **heavens shall pass away** with a great noise, and the **elements shall melt with fervent heat**, the **earth also and the works that are therein shall be burned up** . . .*

*__LOOKING__ for . . . the coming of **the day of God** [the Lord/ Christ], wherein the heavens being on FIRE shall be dissolved, and the elements shall melt with fervent heat?"*

It is obvious that the "Day of the Lord" is the day Jesus comes "as a thief in the night," at His Second Coming to earth. Thus, the Day of the Lord cannot include Daniel's Seventieth Week. It is a totally *separate event* that comes immediately after the Great Tribulation is cut short for the sake of the elect (Matt. 24:22).

Revelation 3:2a-3b:

*"Be WATCHFUL and strengthen the things which remain . . . If therefore thou shalt not __WATCH__, I will come on thee __AS A THIEF__, and thou **shalt not know what hour I will come** upon thee."*

Almost all dispensationalists believe the seven churches of Revelation 2-3 were literal churches that existed in John's day ("which are," Rev. 1:19) and represent church history down through the centuries, sometime *before* the Rapture. The post-trib, "as a thief" phrase is applied to the church of Sardis, which was called the "dead" church in Revelation 3:1.

Sardis had a mix of a few saved members (3:4), but a lot more lost (spiritually dead) members (3:1, 5). This ties in perfectly, consistently, and harmoniously with the parables of Jesus, concerning the wicked servants who are ultimately judged in the end as hypocrites and false brethren when the Lord returns (see Matt. 24:45-51; 25:1-30).

[Note: Mid-Acts or ultra-dispensationalists believe Revelation 2-3 refers *exclusively* to seven literal churches in Turkey (Asia Minor) that will exist during the *future* Great Tribulation. Though tenuous, this novel futurist view rightly affirms the post-trib, "as a thief," coming of the Lord.]

Revelation 16:14-16:

*"For they are the spirits of devils, working miracles, which go forth unto the kings of the earth and of the whole world, to gather them to **the battle of that great DAY OF GOD ALMIGHTY** [i.e., the Day of the Lord].*

*Behold, I come **AS A THIEF**, Blessed is he that **WATCHETH** and keepeth his garments [symbolic of living a holy life], lest he walk naked, and they see his shame. And he gathered them together into a place called in the Hebrew tongue **Armageddon**."*

The great battle of Armageddon is tied in with the coming of Christ "as a thief" at the end of the Great Tribulation. Those who are expecting Christ and living for Him will not be ashamed when He appears.

A Day is as a Thousand Years?

2 Peter 3:8 says, *"one day is with the Lord **as a thousand years**, and a thousand years as one day."* Many dispensationalists from all camps believe this verse suggests that the Day of the Lord includes the millennial Kingdom Age. But that is not scriptural! The Day of the Lord wrath begins at the Second Coming of Christ (see 2 Pet. 2:10-13; Rev. 19:11-21; 20:7-15; 21:1) and lasts for a SINGLE day—*"But it SHALL BE **ONE DAY** which shall be known to the Lord"* (Zech. 14:7 cf. 14:1, 4-6).

Peter was simply referring to the fact that God is very patient because He loves all human beings and is not willing that any should perish, but that all would come to repentance and faith in Jesus

Christ (John 3:16; 2 Peter 3:9). Regardless of one's millennial view (premillennial or amillennial), **the Day of the Lord is NOT the Seventieth Week of Daniel or the Great Tribulation period!** The Day of the Lord is a totally and completely *separate* event that happens immediately *after* the Great Tribulation, right *after the cosmic signs* in the heavens occur (cp. Joel 2:30-31; Matt. 24:29).

The Day of Christ

Having looked at several key portions of Scripture that pertain to the future Day of the Lord, let's now go back and examine "the Day of Christ" (i.e., the Rapture) and see if there is biblical justification to say that it is not the Day of the Lord, but rather, a separate event, as some pretribulationalists teach. 2 Thessalonians 2:1-3 states—

> *"Now we beseech you, brethren, by the **coming of our Lord Jesus Christ**, and by **our gathering together unto him**, that ye be not soon shaken in mind, or be troubled, neither by spirit, nor by word, nor by letter as from us, as that **the day of Christ** is **at hand** [near, imminent, about to happen] . . . **that day shall NOT COME**, except there comes a falling away FIRST and that **man of sin be revealed**."*

The Thessalonians believers were distressed after someone wrote them a false report telling them the *coming of Christ was imminent*, while they were experiencing trials and suffering for their faith in Christ. In other words, they believed the Great Tribulation was upon them. But if they were upset and confused because Paul had taught them they would never enter into the Tribulation, why didn't Paul just come right out and remind them that Christians will never go through it?

Paul did say, *"God hath not appointed us to wrath"* (1 Thess. 5:9), but that does not necessarily mean (nor prove) the church, the body of Christ, cannot or will not go through the Great Tribulation. God's wrath in the Bible is always reserved for apostates and other unrepentant enemies of God, not His children. The truth is, Paul never taught that Christians (the body of Christ) in the last days would be *exempt* from the Tribulation. Rather, he said before the Lord comes back to "gather together" believers at the Day of Christ there would first come a time of great apostasy and then the rise of the Antichrist.

This ties in perfectly with our Lord's teaching in Matthew 24, and Paul's first letter to the Thessalonians, when he told them they should stay awake, watch, and be sober as they wait for the Day of the Lord, when Jesus comes as a thief in the night, to rapture all the Christians and bring destruction upon the world (5:1-9). Paul even said, *"Remember ye not, that, when I was yet with you I told you these things?"* (2 Thess. 2:5). Why would Paul use all the phrases related to the Second Coming of Christ at the end of the Tribulation (e.g., watch, day of the Lord, thief in the night, etc.) and apply it to the Thessalonian believers, if the Day of Christ is not the *same day* as the Day of the Lord (which comes after the Tribulation) or if the church, the body of Christ, won't even be here during the Tribulation?

There is no solid basis to teach that the Day of Christ is not the Day of the Lord. Christ is Lord. They are simply two phrases used interchangeably to identify the "one day" when Jesus comes back at the end of the age, immediately after the Tribulation, to "gather together" His own, and bring wrath upon unbelievers. Any distinction is artificial and tenuous and is used to maintain the wrong idea that Christ is coming back *twice* at the end of the age for two different classes of covenant people—Israel and the Christian Church.

Expectancy vs. Imminency

Christians are to live expectantly as we eagerly look forward to our Lord's return from heaven (as a bride faithfully waits for her husband) after the events of the Tribulation transpire. Jesus told the faithful to "watch" and "be ready" for the Master's return, all in the context of the Second Coming of Christ (Matt. 24:32-51; 25:1-30; Lk. 21:28-32).

Paul pointed the Thessalonians, who were in the body of Christ, to the coming Day of the Lord (or the Day of Christ) as part of their instruction on how to live as they watch and wait for the Lord who will come "as a thief in the night" (1 Thess. 5:1-8). Christians are not to be caught unawares or be surprised at our Lord's coming. Peter also exhorted believers to *look* for the Day of the Lord and a new heaven and new earth, which will come right after the Tribulation, when this present earth shall be burned up and the elements shall melt with intense heat to form a new earth (see 2 Peter 3:10-13).

Remember, several events must take place before the rapture/coming of Christ can occur. Jesus said the gospel would be preached to the whole world before He returns (Matt. 24:14). Obviously that would take much time to accomplish. Jesus also taught many parables of the Kingdom of God/heaven, indicating that His coming would be delayed. The parables of *the tares in the field* (Matt. 13:36-43), *the two servants* (Matt. 24:45-51), *the ten virgins* (Matt. 25:1-13), *the talents* (Matt. 25:14-30), and *the nobleman* (Lk. 19:11-27) all teach that it would take a very long time before the Lord returns.

To say that those parables all pertain to the Second Coming of Christ at the end of the age, hence, do not affect the "any moment" rapture teaching, is illogical and weak. Why would Christ come back to rapture Christians in the first century, for example, only to then delay His Second Coming for 2,000 years? In fact, according to the pre-trib Rapture view, the Antichrist in the last days cannot come on the scene until the Church (which they say is restraining the Antichrist from appearing) is removed in the Rapture (more on this in chapter 6, question 3). This would require that the Rapture be tied in with the Tribulation, after a long delay of our Lord's return, just as Jesus taught.

Paul apparently didn't believe that the coming of Christ was imminent either, as we have seen in his letter to the Thessalonians about the Antichrist. Furthermore, Paul was called to preach the gospel to the Gentiles throughout the Roman Empire. Obviously that would, and did, take many years to accomplish. Paul also predicted he would go to Jerusalem (Acts 20:22), and warned of false teachers that would come and not spare the flock *after* he was gone (Acts 20:29). Hence, Paul definitely was not an "any moment" rapturist! Jesus also foretold that Peter (who was a fairly young man at the time) would be led away and put to death as an old man (Jn. 21:18-19). Peter certainly could not have been an "any moment" rapture teacher either!

Some say Jesus could still have come anytime He liked. I disagree! Why? Because that contradicts the teachings of Jesus and Paul and makes light of Bible prophecy. Jesus cannot come back from heaven any ol' time He likes, but only when the Father sends Him forth to accomplish His divine purpose, in the exact order that He has decreed. In short, Jesus is not playing any moment "tag" with the church in these last days. There is an orderly divine plan going on and everyone needs to take God's salvation plan seriously (i.e., repent and believe the gospel—1 Corinthians 15:1-4) so they can be ready when Christ does come back, according to divine schedule.

Furthermore, it would take much time to develop the world empires foretold in Bible prophecy before the end would come, such as the revived Roman Empire, i.e., the European ten-nation confederacy led by the Antichrist (Dan. 2:1-45; 9:26-27; Rev. 13), Russia and the Arab league of nations (Ezek. 38-39), and the Asian "Kings of the East," 200 million-man army (Rev. 9:16; 16:12).

Military technology, the worldwide unification of commerce and banking (Rev. 13), the worldwide dispersion of the Jews in A.D. 70, and the eventual rebirth of national Israel (in 1948) in the last days has all taken hundreds of years to transpire (Ezek. 38:8; Luke 21:24). Also, the worldwide apostasy (falling away from God and truth) and ever-worsening moral condition of mankind, even within the church (1 Tim. 3:1-10; Rev. 3:14-19), and the Christ-rejecting scoffers that shall come in the last days (2 Pet. 3:3-4). And finally, the mystery Babylon ecumenical religion, led most likely by the papacy in Vatican City, Rome (the city that sits on seven hills), in the last days (Rev. 17-18) would take much time to develop too. They all play a critical role in the final end-time scenario.

Much more could be written but suffice it to say, **the "any moment" and "signless" rapture teaching is a <u>FALSE</u> teaching, plain and simple**. Expectancy is the proper biblical attitude that Christians in every generation should have as we watch and wait for the return of our Lord from heaven. When the "signs of the times" that Jesus gave in Matthew 24 come to pass, and the Gentile (heathen) nations begin to assemble their armies in the valley of Jehoshaphat, in Israel, then, *and only then*, will His return be imminent (Joel 3:12-16; Rev. 16:14-16).

[For more information, read Part I in this prophecy trilogy: *Signs of the Second Coming of Jesus Christ and the End of the World*.]

Fundamentalism's Tie with Dispensationalism

John Nelson Darby (father of the modern dispensational movement) and C.I. Scofield were the two most influential Christians (both were fundamentalist authors and powerful speakers) who were instrumental in the founding and promoting of dispensational theology and the "any moment" Rapture. In fact, leading fundamentalists today claim that had these men, along with other great fundamentalist leaders early on (such as A. J. Gordon, James H. Brooks, A. C. Gaebelein, and A. T. Pierson), rejected dispensationalism and its key distinctives, fundamentalism would not exist in its present form.[1] But it seems odd that such a supposedly obvious teaching as dispensationalism claims to be (if one takes a literal interpretation of Scripture), that we needed these men to show it to us after almost nineteen hundred years of church history.

The truth is, the "any moment" (imminent), *pre-trib* Rapture teaching is not an obvious doctrine in the New Testament (such as the virgin birth of Christ and His deity, atonement, and bodily resurrection)! Modern dispensationalism is, in all likelihood, a misinterpretation of Scripture, well systemized by certain sincere fundamentalist brethren, and has become widely spread through very popular Christian teachers and every possible means available (e.g., radio, TV, pulpit, print, tapes, videos, CDs, DVDs, prophecy seminars, the Internet, and so on).

[1] Three key distinctives of Acts 2 Dispensationalism are:
1. Israel and the Church are completely separate and distinct. The church age is a parenthetical time, from Pentecost (Acts 2) to the Rapture, when God deals primarily with the Gentiles, not the Jews (Israel).
2. The secret, any-moment, "pre-trib" Rapture.
3. Premillennial return of Christ to a world that will not get better as we near the end of the age, but only worse, with great apostasy in the church, just before Christ sets up His literal theocratic kingdom on earth, along with Levite priests and sin offerings (animal sacrifices) reinstituted (Ezek. 40-48).

Conclusion

The Day of the Lord/Christ is a unique, single, "day" that clearly happens immediately after the Great Tribulation at the Second

Coming of Christ. It starts with the cosmic signs in the heavens and then the Rapture of the saints and the revelation (revealing) of Jesus Christ from heaven, back-to-back, when He comes openly and visibly, in flaming fire, to bring wrath upon an unrepentant world of sinners (2 Thess. 1:7-10).

When the Tribulation signs of Matthew 24 and 2 Thessalonians 2 actually do take place, especially when the death toll of the human race mounts to near annihilation (Matt. 24:22; Mark 13:20), and the armies of the world assembly at Armageddon (the valley of Jehoshaphat) in Israel (Joel 3:11-16; Rev. 16:14-16), *then* the Lord's coming (*parousia,* singular), at the end of this present age, will become imminent (near). Christians are commanded by both Jesus and Paul to watch for the key prophetic signs that indicate the Lord's coming is near, so we may never be deceived by anyone who claims the Lord has arrived or is about to arrive before divine schedule (2 Thess. 2:1-3). Knowing this can literally save one's own life in the future Tribulation!

> *"Then if they shall say unto you, Behold, he is in the desert;* **GO NOT FORTH***; behold he is in the secret chambers;* **BELIEVE IT NOT***. For* **AS LIGHTNING COMETH** *OUT OF THE EAST, and SHINETH [the shekinah glory of Christ] EVEN UNTO THE WEST;* **so shall the** *[visible]* **coming of the Son of man be"** (Matt. 24:26-27).

It will be no secret when the Lord Jesus returns. After a total blackout of the universe, the sign of Christ's coming will then light up the entire skies, and the earth will be shaken with a mighty earthquake and the heavens will split wide open with a sonic boom! Jesus will then appear lightning fast, in flaming fire, with His mighty angels (Joel 3:16; Matt. 24:29; 2 Thess. 2:7-10; 2 Pet. 3:10; Rev. 6:12-17; 16:18).

Remember, Jesus Christ is not merely a resurrected man. He is <u>Lord</u> <u>God</u> Almighty! Zechariah 14:5 says, *"the **Lord** [Yahweh] **my God shall come**, and all the saints with him"* (cf. Rev. 1:7-8). The whole world will know it is Him because "every eye will <u>see</u> <u>him</u>" coming in the clouds, in power and great glory (Matt. 24:30). It will be utterly and totally awesome!! The King of kings and Lord of lords (19:11-16), returning in all His divine glory! There is none other day like it, nor shall there ever be again.

When the key signs of the Great Tribulation begin to come to pass, then we can lift up our heads, knowing the time of our Lord's coming is near, even at the door (Luke 21:28; 1 Thess. 5:1-11). Knowing all this, that God will certainly come and judge the world, Christians ought to live in a manner that is in keeping with godliness (2 Pet. 3:11-12), so we will not be ashamed when our Lord returns (1 Jn. 2:28). All Christians must stand before the Judgment Seat of Christ and give an account to God for what they have said (Matt. 12:36) and done with their lives after their conversion, all for the purpose of receiving praise and rewards from God, position of honor, and privileges of further responsibility in the future kingdom of God (see Matt. 25:14-23; 1 Cor. 3:11-15; 2 Cor. 5:9-10).

All the Old Testament prophets, Jesus, and all the New Testament apostles were completely unified on these matters, thus Christians today ought to be unified on it too.

The Biblical View of Imminency

1. The Beginning of Sorrows (Matt. 24:4-12)
    - Wars and Rumors of Wars
    - Distress Among the Nations
    - The Great Apostasy (falling away) from the Christian Faith (2 Thess. 2:3a)

2. The Great Tribulation (Matt. 24:15-26)
    - The Revealing of the "Man of Sin" (the Antichrist) in the Jewish Temple (2 Thess. 2:3-9)
    - 42 Months of Great Tribulation (Rev. 13:5)
    - Mass Martyrdom of Christians (Rev. 13:7, 15)

3. The Imminent Return of Christ (Matt. 24:14, 22, 29)
    - Gospel Preached to all Nations
    - All the Armies of the Nations Gathered Together to Battle at Armageddon, in Israel (Rev. 16:14-16)
    - Near Annihilation of the Human Race
    - Cosmic Signs in the Heavens (Rev. 6:12-14)

4. Second Coming of Christ as a Thief (Matt. 24:30-31)
    - The Rapture (our gathering together to be with the Lord in the air—1 Thess. 4:15-17; 5:2-9)
    - The Day of the Lord Wrath (Joel 3:12-16; 2 Thess. 2:7-10; 2:8; Rev. 6:15-17; 14:14-20; 16:14-20; 19:11)

5

The Rapture and the Second Coming of Christ

There is coming a day when one generation of human beings will not have to experience death. It is the last generation of Christians who are alive on earth the day Jesus Christ comes back to gather together His own to be with Him forever. 1 Corinthians 15:51-53 states:

*"Behold, I show you a mystery; We shall not all sleep [die], but we shall all be changed, in a moment, in the twinkling of an eye, **at the <u>LAST</u> <u>TRUMP</u>** [cp. Rev. 11:15]: for the trumpet shall sound, and **the dead shall be raised** incorruptible, and **we shall be changed.** For this corruptible [aging, rotten, sinful body] must **put on incorruption,** and this mortal [body] must **put on immortality."***

*"For this we say unto you by the Word of the Lord, that we which are alive and remain unto the **coming** [parousia] **of the Lord** shall not prevent them which are asleep [those that died in Christ].*

*For the Lord himself shall descend from heaven with a shout, with the voice of **the archangel, and with the trump of***

> **God: and the dead in Christ shall rise first: Then we which
> are ALIVE and remain** *[on the earth]* **shall be <u>CAUGHT UP</u>**
> *[raptured]* **<u>TOGETHER WITH THEM</u> <u>IN</u> <u>THE</u> <u>CLOUDS</u>,**
> *to meet the Lord in the air: and so shall we ever be with the
> Lord"* (1 Thess. 4:15-17).

This event has also been called the Rapture [Latin: *raptus*], which means to be "caught up" or carried away. It will be one of the most fantastic and blessed events ever to happen for Christians. Imagine *bypassing death* and instantly receiving a perfect glorified body that cannot sin, nor get hurt or sick, or age, or ever die. A body that can travel faster than light across the universe, has a mind greater than any genius that ever lived, and continues in holy perfection for all eternity. It will be absolutely wonderful! But it is only for those who repent (change their mind and turn to God) and trust in Jesus Christ as their risen Lord and Savior.

When the Rapture comes, and believers have entered their eternal rest, then the saying will come to pass, *"Death is swallowed up in victory. O death, where is thy sting? O grave, where is your victory?"*

Will there really be a Rapture?

There are many false religions, heretical sects, and dead churches today that deny there is going to be a rapture (instant gathering and catching up) of all the saved at the coming of Jesus. They scoff at the Rapture teaching, calling it a foolish "fly-away" escape theory. In fact, many of these apostates deny or doubt the Lord will ever come back again at all!

Peter warned: *"Knowing this first, that there shall come in the last days scoffers, walking after their own lusts, and saying, Where is the promise of his coming?"* (2 Pet. 3:3-4a cf. Acts 1:11).

But as we have seen, the Bible clearly teaches Jesus will return someday and there will indeed be a gathering together of the elect in Christ, in the clouds, at His visible coming at the end of the age. To deny that is to deny the plain teachings of Scripture! Paul made it absolutely crystal clear that at the coming of the Lord, after the dead in Christ are resurrected first, *"then we which are alive and remain shall be **CAUGHT UP** [raptured] **together with them IN THE <u>CLOUDS</u> to meet the Lord IN THE <u>AIR</u>"*** (1 Thess. 4:17).

Some unbelievers like to argue, saying the word "rapture" is not found in the Bible. But the word means to be "caught up." It simply refers to our gathering together to be with the Lord at the end of the age, plain and simple. Only a schismatic heretic (divisive false teacher), willfully ignorant, or spiritually blind person would refuse, or not be able to see, the clear and simple truth of the Rapture (i.e., the Lord Jesus will literally return in the clouds to gather together His own at the end of the age). It is a Bible doctrine that requires spiritual discernment and faith in the Word of God (see 1 Cor. 2:13-14). This does not mean one must believe in a particular view pertaining to its *timing* (such as pre or post-trib) in order to be orthodox (as some wrongly insist), but that Christ will surely return one day to gather His elect to be with Him.

Keep in mind, the doctrine of the Second Coming of Jesus Christ is a fundamental teaching of Christianity and is nonnegotiable.[1] Scores of Old and New Testament prophecies major on it. However, the doctrine of the Rapture itself was a mystery not fully disclosed until Paul expounded on it in his epistles. The mysterious thing about it was not that there would be a resurrection of the dead when Christ returns on the "last day" (Jn. 6:40), but rather, Christians *who are alive* at the Lord's coming would bypass death and be instantly changed into their glorified immortal bodies, and raised up together with those who had previously died. In short, the resurrection and rapture of believers are one and the same event. This means that

Christ's second coming and the Rapture are not necessarily separate events that happen several years or months apart, but that both events will definitely happen.

[Note: Beware of false religious teachers who reject or are in error about any major teaching in the Bible. Usually, if they are wrong in one fundamental teaching of the Bible, they will also reject other important teachings in the Bible, such as the doctrines of the salvation by grace via faith in the gospel of Jesus Christ, the eternal security of the believer, the Trinity, the deity of Christ and His bodily resurrection, the visible and physical Second Coming of Jesus Christ to earth in the future, and/or heaven for all believers and a literal, eternal burning hell for unbelievers. They are usually very rigid and legalistic or they are covetous and greedy and/or sexually immoral. The Bible says to "mark them" and "avoid them" and have "no fellowship" with them, but rather, reprove and expose them (Rom. 16:17-18; 2 Cor. 6:14-17; Eph. 5:11; 2 Tim. 4:2-5; 2 John 9-11). For more information, read the author's book, *Major Cults and False World Religions*.]

[1] The Lord Jesus Christ will gloriously, visibly, and triumphantly return to earth at the end of the age, to defeat Satan and all his minions, resurrect the dead, judge the world, and reign as King in His kingdom, and as the Lamb, forever (Dan. 2:44; 7:13-14; Zech. 14:3-9; Matt. 25:31-46; Mk. 13:6; Lk. 1:31-33; Jn. 5:27-29; 6:40; 1 Cor. 15:23-25, 51-52; 2 Thess. 1:7-10; 2:8; Rev. 1:7; 11:15; 19:11-16; 20:10-15; 21:1-3, 22; 22:3-5).

Four Main Rapture Views

Although all true Christians believe Jesus Christ will come to gather His own, not all are agreed as to the timing. There are four main rapture views that dispensationalists hold to:

1. Pre-trib Rapture: Christ comes in **two phases**—once *before* the 70th Week of Daniel to rapture the Church in the air and *take her back to heaven for seven years* and marries her. Jesus returns to earth with His bride right after the Great Tribulation at His Second Coming.

Rapture (Beginning of Sorrows)	2nd Coming of Christ
3 1/2 years of pseudo peace	3 1/2 years of Great Tribulation
Daniel's 70th Week (7 years long)	

2. Mid-trib Rapture: Christ comes in **two phases**—once at about the *middle* of the 70th Week of Daniel to rapture the Church in the air and *take her back to heaven*, just before the three and one-half years (42 months) of Great Tribulation begins. Jesus returns to earth with His bride right *after* the Great Tribulation at His Second Coming.

Antichrist Comes **Rapture**	2nd Coming of Christ
1st half of Daniel's 70th Week	42 Months of Great Tribulation

3. Pre-wrath Rapture: Christ comes in **two phases**—*immediately after the Great Tribulation is cut short*, about three-quarters of the way through the 70th Week of Daniel, to rapture the Church in the air and *take her back to heaven* to *reward believers at the Bema Seat of Christ.* Jesus returns to earth with His bride after the prolonged **Day of the Lord's wrath** is poured out upon the world for about **18-21 months.**

Newly Rebuilt Jewish Temple Antichrist in Temple	2nd Coming/**Rapture** The Great Tribulation	Day of the Lord Wrath
1st half of Daniel's 70th Week	The Trib cut short on DOL	18-21 mos.

4. Post-trib Rapture: Christ comes only <u>once</u>, immediately *after* the Great Tribulation to gather together (rapture) His own in the air. Then the **Day of the Lord (DOL)** wrath begins and lasts for **ONE DAY**, when Jesus returns with His saints to deliver Israel at the battle of Armageddon and set up His kingdom on earth at His Second Coming.

Antichrist makes 7-year covenant Antichrist breaks covenant	2nd Coming/**Rapture** The Great Tribulation	Day of the Lord
1st half of Daniel's 70th Week (42 Months)	The Tribulation cut short at the DOL (the Last Day)	One Day

A Brief Overview

The mid-trib and pre-wrath Rapture views are not very popular or well-known (or entirely scriptural), but both need to be discussed somewhat.

The mid-trib view rightly sees that certain signs are required to happen before the Rapture can happen. But it fails to see that the Day of the Lord wrath (which comes immediately after the Trib) is separate and distinct from the Tribulation judgments; thus, errs by assuming that the Church (true Christians) will be removed before the Great Tribulation occurs. Many mid-trib teachers believe in the unity of the saints of all ages, yet they hold to two separate comings of Christ for the people of God—one at the Rapture and the other at the end of the Great Tribulation. The coming of Christ is viewed as a two-phase, 3 1/2 year coming, which contradicts the short, single-phase coming in Matthew 24:29-31.

The pre-wrath Rapture is a recent and fairly commendable view that got started around 1990, in America, by a former pre-trib Rapture speaker and writer, Marv Rosenthal (Zion's Hope). It correctly teaches the Day of the Lord comes *immediately after* the Tribulation, but fails to see that the Day of the Lord is very brief, probably a literal solar day long (though it could be a little longer, since it is a unique day). This affects the chronological order of the trumpet and bowl judgments in relation to the seal judgments in the book of Revelation. When the *sixth* seal is opened in Revelation 6:12, the Day of the Lord begins. After that, the trumpet and bowl judgments continue to run *consecutively* in the pre-wrath scheme, during the *extended time* of the Day of the Lord. Posttribulationalism views the intensifying seal, trumpet, and bowl judgments happening *concurrently* (in overlays), all converging at the single "Day" of the Lord (cp. Rev. 6:12-17; 11:15-18; 16:15-19).

The pre-wrath view says the church is taken *back to heaven* and rewarded at the Bema-Seat of Christ during the Day of the Lord (which lasts for about 21 months) and then returns with Christ to earth afterwards. This results in a *double* coming of Christ, even though the pre-wrath view stresses there is only a *single* coming of Christ at the end of the age. However, the Bible does not necessarily teach we are taken back to heaven when Jesus returns. Rather, Jesus brings His reward *with Him* when He comes back to save believers and judge mankind (Jn. 14:2-3; 2 Thess. 1:7-10; Rev. 7:15-17; 11:18; 21:1-5; 22:12).

The pre-wrath view is a blend between the mid-trib and post-trib views, the main difference being *the length of the Day of the Lord* after the Rapture. But it is really closer to posttribulationalism because it correctly recognizes the unity of all the saints of all ages being "in Christ" and the post-trib coming of the Lord to rapture the church, immediately after the "cut short" (shortened) tribulation period. (Practically, it really does not matter much whether one holds to pre-wrath or post-trib view because both see the church going through the Great Tribulation and experiencing persecution and martyrdom).

As for the pre-trib view, pretribulationalists see much discontinuity (division) in the plan of God between Israel and the Church and this affects a lot of other doctrines, as we have previously seen. They say the next event on the prophetic calendar is the "any moment" Rapture, and that it is a signless event, even though this clearly contradicts the teachings of both Jesus in Matthew 24 and Paul in 2 Thessalonians 2:1-3. Acts 2 pretribulationalism also sees the New Testament church as being the *exclusive* "bride of Christ," which also contradicts Scripture. Imminency (any moment Rapture) and exclusivity of the New Testament church (they say the church, the body of Christ, began at Pentecost) are the two main pillars of pretribulationalism.

Pretribulationalism says when the Rapture occurs millions of people will suddenly be gone, nowhere to be found. The world will then go into total panic! Husbands, wives, family, friends, children, and babies mysteriously snatched away. Was it by aliens? Unknown forces? God? The headlines in the following morning newspapers will read:

MILLIONS MISSING!

But the truth is, THERE WILL BE <u>NO</u> <u>NEWSPAPERS</u> THE DAY AFTER CHRIST'S RETURN! Right after the Rapture, the Day of the Lord will commence, bringing total destruction upon the whole world in a single day (1 Thess. 5:2-3; 2 Peter 3:10-12; Rev. 18:8).

Which Rapture teaching is right?

To determine which Rapture view most closely fits the biblical teaching, one needs to do a lot of careful Scripture comparison, starting with the more obvious and clear texts. That is the key to interpreting any subject in the Bible. Therefore, if we examine the most obvious teachings that pertain to the Rapture first, we can then, through a process of elimination, sort out the true from the false. Remember, all four views can't be right! Only one view rightly divides the Word of God.

To begin with, it seems rather obvious that Jesus and Paul both taught there were signs that would have to come to pass before the Rapture and the Second Coming of Christ would occur—a major one being the revealing of the Antichrist in the last days (Matt.

24:15; 2 Thess. 2:3). This strikes a major blow to the pre-trib Rapture theory.

The second obvious teaching in the Bible is that Christians are commanded to "watch" and be ready for the coming of the Lord who will come "as a thief in the night" on the Day of the Lord, which comes immediately *after* the Tribulation (Matt. 24:29-31; 1 Thess 5:2-9). This automatically strikes another major blow to the pre-trib Rapture theory and now to the mid-trib Rapture theory.

The third obvious teaching in the Bible is that the Day of the Lord not only comes immediately after the Great Tribulation, but it is also very brief and lasts only "one day," when Jesus comes back to earth to defend Jerusalem at His visible Second Coming (see Zech. 14:1, 4, 6-7; Matt. 24:30; 1 Thess. 5:2-3; 2 Thess. 1:7-10; Rev. 6:12-17; 11:15-18; 14:8, 20; 16:15-16; 18:8, 10, 19; 19:11-16).

This automatically strikes a third major blow to the pre-trib Rapture theory, a second major blow to the mid-trib Rapture theory, and now a major blow to the pre-wrath Rapture theory, which says the Day of the Lord lasts for an extended time period of several months, while the saints who were raptured are back in heaven being rewarded. This leaves the post-trib Rapture view as the only viable teaching that consistently harmonizes with the Bible, concerning all prophetic events.

[Note: Pre and midtribulationalism assumes that the parousia (coming) of Christ is a two-phase coming, based on the idea that the Old Testament prophecies concerning the coming Messiah were two-fold—first, as a sin-bearer (lamb), and second, as a mighty king to make war at the end of the age. But to then teach that the Second Coming of Christ must also be a two-fold coming is an assumption, all based on scriptural silence! Jesus clearly taught that His coming at the end of the age is going to be a brief, single event, and absolutely nothing in Paul's teachings contradicts that.]

Main Rapture and Second Coming Verses

Having established the very likely fact that the posttribulational Rapture is the correct view, let's now pull together several key verses in the New Testament in chronological order that are related to the Rapture and the Second Coming of Christ, and see how Jesus and the apostles Paul, Peter, and John were all in complete harmony and unity with each other in their eschatological (future events) teachings.

Observe the repeated phrases and key words in the following verses, such as—*coming as a thief, watch, be ready, mighty angels, flaming fire, last trumpet, wrath, gather together, day of the Lord/ Christ/God, I come quickly.* All these phrases intertwine throughout scripture and are used to describe the single, *posttribulational* Rapture and the Second Coming of Jesus Christ.

[Note: One of the key principles of Bible interpretation is comparing scripture with scripture, looking for repetitious words and phrases that indicate that an event is one and the same in all related Bible passages.]

Jesus

Matthew 24:29-31:

*"Immediately **AFTER THE TRIBULATION** of those days shall the **sun be darkened, and moon shall not give her ligh**t, and the **stars shall fall from heaven** . . . Then shall appear the sign [epiphany] of the Son of man in heaven . . . and they shall **SEE the Son of man coming in the clouds** of heaven with power and great glory.*

*And he shall send his **angels** with a great **sound of a TRUMPET** and they shall **GATHER TOGETHER his ELECT** from the four winds, from one end of heaven to the other."*

Matthew 24:36-44:

*"But of **that day and hour** [i.e., the Second Advent of Jesus Christ] knoweth no man, no, not the angels of heaven, but my Father only. But as the days of Noah were, so shall also the **coming** [parousia, singular] **of the Son of man be**.*

*For as in the days that were before the flood they were eating and drinking, marrying and giving in marriage, until the day that Noah <u>entered into the ark</u> . . . Then shall two be in the field: the **one shall be taken**, and **the other left** . . .*

*<u>**WATCH**</u> therefore: for ye know not what hour your Lord doth come. But know this, that if the goodman of the house had known in what watch the **<u>THIEF</u>** would come, he would have watched, and would not suffered his house to be broken up. Therefore **BE YE ALSO <u>READY</u>**: for in such **an hour as ye think not the Son of man cometh**."*

Some say that the "one taken" in Matthew 24:40 is taken in the Rapture and the "other left" is left for judgment because Noah and his family were taken (or gathered together) in the Ark of safety (a type of Christ) above the deadly flood waters that came upon the whole earth. Others hold that the "one taken" is taken away in judgment (represented by the flood) and the other one is left to repopulate the earthly kingdom during the future Millennium (just as the survivors in the Ark did afterwards). Regardless, it does not matter which view is right because the context of Matthew 24:27-51 is all about the post-trib coming of Jesus Christ at the end of the age.

Matthew 25:5, 6, 8-13:

*"While **the bridegroom TARRIED**, they [the ten virgins] all slumbered and slept. And at midnight there was a cry made, Behold, the bridegroom cometh; go ye out to meet him . . . And the foolish [five virgins] said unto the wise, Give us of your oil; for our lamps have gone out. But the wise answered, saying, Not so; lest there be*

not enough for us and you: but go ye rather to them that sell, and buy for yourselves.

*And while they went to buy, the bridegroom came, and **they that were READY** went in [the kingdom] with him to **THE MARRIAGE** and the door was shut. Afterward came also the other virgins, saying, Lord, Lord, open to us. But he answered and said, Verily I say unto you, **I know you NOT**. **WATCH** therefore, for ye know neither **the day nor the hour** wherein the **Son of man cometh**."*

The marriage represents salvation, plain and simple. The wise virgins represent the people of God (Israel first) which are saved and ready to meet the Lord, and will enter into the marriage of the Lamb and the celebration supper at His coming. All this results in *all believers* inheriting the kingdom and eternal life (cf. Matt. 25:34; Rev. 19:7-9). The unprepared foolish virgins represent the lost whom Jesus does not know as His own at His sudden coming and will be told to depart into the *eternal* lake of fire (cf. Matt. 7:21-23; 25:41; Rev. 20:11-15).

Luke 21:28, 31:

*"And when these things begin to come to pass [the events of the Great Tribulation], **then look up**, and lift up your heads; for your redemption [deliverance by Jesus at His Second Coming] **draweth nigh** . . .*

*So likewise ye, **when ye SEE THESE THINGS come to pass, KNOW ye that the kingdom of God is nigh** [near] **at hand** [imminent, about to happen]."*

Luke 21:34-36:

*"**And take heed to yourselves**, lest at any time your hearts be overcharged with **surfeiting** [excessive eating and drinking, debauchery, partying] **and drunkenness**, and **cares of this life**, and so **that DAY***

come upon you UNAWARES. For as a snare shall it [the Tribulation] come on all them that dwell on the face of the whole earth.

WATCH ye therefore, and pray always, that ye may be accounted worthy [or have the courage, strength, and discernment] to escape all these things [especially the Jews living in Israel at that time] that shall come to pass [the temptations and deadly traps of the Tribulation—Matt. 24:15-26; Mk. 13:14-23, 34-37; Rev. 12:6], and to stand before the Son of man [as a faithful overcomer and wise servant at His second coming]."

[Note: There are some who hold to a "partial rapture" theory based on Luke 21:34-36. They think it means that only some Christians will be "worthy" to be raptured and escape the Tribulation because they were faithfully living for God. The other Christians are supposedly left behind to go through the Tribulation because they were living sinfully in their conduct, and thus, must be chastened, in order to bring them to holiness. But that contradicts Paul's teaching. He said there is just one coming of Christ at the end and *all* Christians will be raised up together (1 Cor. 15:23), not just some. Carnal (lazy, sinning, lukewarm) believers will suffer loss and be ashamed at the Judgment Seat of Christ (1 Cor. 3:10-15; 2 Cor. 5:9-10). But no Christian will miss the Rapture. Remember, the context of Luke 21 is about the single, *posttribulational* coming of the Lord.]

John 14:2-3:

"In my Father's house are many mansions [dwelling places]: if it were not so, I would have told you. I go to prepare a place for you. And if I go and prepare a place for you, I WILL COME AGAIN, and receive you unto myself; that where I am, there ye may be also."

Many dispensationalists believe this is one passage that refers to Christians being taken *back to heaven* with Jesus at the Rapture, to dwell there while the Tribulation is taking place on the earth. However, only two days earlier, in the Olivet Discourse, Jesus taught

His disciples about His coming, which they would have understood to happen right *after* of the Great Tribulation (see Matthew 24:31).

Jesus does not tell His disciples He will take them back to heaven when He returns, only to vacate it seven short years later. When Jesus comes, *they will remain with Him* and He is bringing His reward with Him, including the heavenly New Jerusalem (Mount Zion), the eternal city of God (Heb. 11:10; 12:22; 13:14; Rev. 3:12; 21:2) that will come down out of heaven on the Day of the Lord, when the present heavens and earth are burned up, cleansed, and melted down to make a new heavens and a new earth (cp. Isa. 65:17-25; 66:22-23; Acts 3:21; Heb. 12:26-28; 2 Pet. 3:10-13; 21:1-5). The saints will then dwell in mansions in the holy city with the Lord forever (Rev. 7:14-18; 21:2-3).

[Note: Regardless of one's view, John 14:2-3 does not clearly teach a *pre-trib* or *imminent* rapture, but only that Jesus will return to take His own to be with Him.]

Paul

1 Corinthians 15:22-24:

*"For as in Adam all die, even so **in Christ** shall all be made alive. But every man in his own order: **Christ the firstfruits** [at his resurrection]; afterward **they that are Christ's at his coming** [parousia].*

*   **Then cometh THE END**, when he shall have delivered up **the** [present mystery form of the] **kingdom to God**, even the Father; when he shall have put down all rule and all authority and power."*

1 Corinthians 15:51-52:

*"Behold, I show you a mystery; We shall not all sleep [die], but we shall all be changed, in a moment, in the twinkling [1/40 of a second] of an eye, **AT THE LAST TRUMP**; for the trumpet shall sound, and*

the **DEAD IN CHRIST** *shall be RAISED INCORRUPTIBLE, and we shall be changed."*

Paul makes it clear that after the bodily resurrection of Jesus (1 Cor. 15:3-8), who was the firstborn from the dead (vs. 20), there is to be only ONE resurrection, not two, of the saints at the post-trib coming of Christ. This includes the redeemed OT saints (Dan. 12:2) and the church age saints (1 Thess. 4:15-17), which includes the Trib saints (Rev. 20:4). Thus, all the saints of all time are raised up incorruptible at that point. Then comes "the end" when Christ defeats His enemies at the battle of Armageddon and sets up His everlasting kingdom, and reigns forever and ever (Rev. 11:15 cp. Dan. 7:13-14, 18).

1 Thessalonians 1:10:

*"And to **wait** for his Son from heaven, whom he raised from the dead, even Jesus which **delivered us from the <u>WRATH</u> to come**."*

[Note: Many Christians equate God's "wrath" as being the Great Tribulation. But wrath in the Bible is also related to the Day of the Lord afterwards and the final perdition of the ungodly in Hell (Jn. 3:36; 2 Pet. 3:7-10; Rev. 14:11; 21:8).]

1 Thessalonians 4:15-17:

*"For this we say unto you by the Word of the Lord, that we which are alive and remain unto the **coming** [parousia] of the Lord shall not prevent them which are asleep [those that died in Christ].*

*For the Lord himself shall descend from heaven with a shout, with the voice of **<u>the archangel</u>, and with the <u>trump of God</u>: and the dead in Christ shall rise first: Then we which are ALIVE and remain shall be <u>CAUGHT UP</u> TOGETHER with them in THE CLOUDS,** to meet the Lord in the air: and so shall we ever be with the Lord."*

1 Thessalonians 5:1-4, 6, 9:

*"But of the times and the seasons [leading up to the Day of the Lord], brethren, ye have no need that I write unto you. For yourselves [Christians] know perfectly that the **DAY OF THE LORD** so cometh **AS A THIEF IN THE NIGHT**.*

*For when they shall say, Peace and safety; then sudden **destruction** cometh upon them, as travail upon a woman with child; and they shall not escape. But ye, brethren, are not in darkness, that **that day** should overtake you **AS A THIEF** [or by surprise] . . . Therefore let us not sleep, as do others; but **let us WATCH** [for the key signs that indicate His coming is near] and **be sober** . . . for God hath **not appointed us to WRATH** [the final destruction and perdition of the wicked] but to obtain salvation [deliverance] by our Lord Jesus Christ"* (cf. Matt. 24:42-51, the illustration of the wise servant vs. the drunken evil servant).

2 Thessalonians 1:7, 8, 10:

*"And to you who are troubled rest with us, when the Lord Jesus shall be REVEALED [Gr: apokalypsis] FROM HEAVEN with his mighty **ANGELS**, in FLAMING **FIRE** taking **VENGEANCE** [or wrath] on them that know not God, and that obey not the gospel of our Lord Jesus Christ . . . when he shall **come** [at the end of the age] to be glorified in his saints, and to be admired in all them that believe (because our testimony among you was believed) in **THAT DAY**."*

2 Thessalonians 2:1-5:

*"Now we beseech you, brethren, by **the coming of our Lord Jesus Christ**, and by **our gathering together** [the Rapture] **unto him**, that ye be not soon shaken in mind, or be troubled [nervously anxious], neither by spirit, nor by word, nor by letter as from us, as*

that ***the day of Christ*** *[or day of the Lord]* ***is at hand*** *[near, imminent, impending, about to happen].*

Let no man deceive you by any means: for ***that day*** *[the Rapture]* **shall NOT come**, *except there* **come a falling away** *[apostasy or religious defection and rebellion against God]* **FIRST**, *and that* <u>**MAN OF SIN**</u> *[the Antichrist]* <u>**BE REVEALED**</u>, *the son of perdition.*

Who opposeth and exalteth himself above all that is called God, or that is worshipped; so ***that he as God sitteth in the temple of God***, showing himself that he is God [see Matt. 24:15]. Remember ye not, that, when I was yet with you, I told you these things?"

[Note: It is unlikely the *apostasia* (apostasy or departure) of 2:3 refers to the Rapture. The context points to a falling away or defection from the faith (2:10 cf. 1 Tim. 4:1; 2 Tim. 3:1). See chapter 6, question 4.]

Philippians 3:20-21:

"For our conversation [or citizenship] is in heaven; from whence also we <u>***LOOK***</u> ***for the Saviour, the Lord Jesus Christ,*** *Who shall* ***change our vile body***, *that it may be fashioned like unto his glorious body, according to the working whereby he is able even to subdue all things unto himself."*

Titus 2:13:

"<u>***LOOKING***</u> *for* ***that blessed hope*** *[the coming of Jesus], and the* ***glorious*** *[the shekina glory of God]* ***APPEARING*** *[Gr: epiphaneia] of the great God and our Savior Jesus Christ."*

[Note: There are those who say that by teaching that the church is to look for signs that signal the return of Christ and our gathering together to be with the Lord at the Rapture (i.e., those signs listed in Matthew 24 and 2 Thessalonians 2), means the church then is not looking for Jesus but for the Antichrist! They then claim that is not the Blessed Hope, but rather, the blasted hope! This leaves the false impression that the Tribulation

Christians are going to be betrayed by their Lord and have no true hope! But the believer's "hope" is not in *avoiding* physical death. The *Blessed Hope* of every Christian is the COMING OF JESUS, no matter when it happens. When Jesus comes, He will bring His reward with Him (Rev. 22:12) and all God's people will be in His presence forevermore.]

Hebrews 9:27-28 (assuming Paul wrote Hebrews):

*"And as it is appointed unto men ONCE to die, but after this the judgment; So Christ was **ONCE** offered to bear the sins of many; and unto them that **LOOK FOR HIM** shall he appear the **SECOND TIME** without sin unto salvation."*

No mention of a third coming of Christ.

Peter

2 Peter 3:10-13:

*"But the **DAY OF THE LORD** will come **AS A THIEF** IN THE NIGHT; in the which the heavens shall pass away with a great noise, and the **elements shall melt with fervent heat**, the **earth also and the works that are therein shall be burned up**.*

Seeing then that all these things shall be dissolved, what manner of persons ought ye to be in all holy conversation and godliness.

***LOOKING** for and hasting unto the coming of **the day of God** [the Lord/Christ], wherein the heavens being on **FIRE** shall be dissolved, and the elements shall melt with fervent heat? Nevertheless we, according to his promise, **LOOK FOR NEW HEAVENS** and a **NEW EARTH**, wherein dwelleth righteousness"* (cf. Rev. 21-22).

It is obvious the Day of the Lord, which is the Second Coming of Christ, brings on the new heavens and new earth at that time, not one thousand years later, as our premillennial brethren teach. That is also when the New Jerusalem city comes down to dwell with mankind.

[For more information about the present and future kingdom of God, the New Jerusalem, and various millennial views, read the author's book: *Nowmillennial Dispensationalism (A Biblical Examination of the Millennium and the Kingdom of God)*.]

John

1 John 2:28:

"And now, little children, abide in him; that, when he shall appear, we may have confidence, and NOT BE ASHAMED before him AT HIS COMING."

At the coming of Christ, all Christians will stand before the judgment (bema) seat of Christ to give an account of their stewardship before God and have their life works examined for rewards (Rom. 14:10, 12; 2 Cor. 5:9-10).

Salvation is a free gift and cannot be earned (Eph. 2:8-9). However, Christians can *earn* rewards for their service to God *after* they become saved and are, in fact, commanded to do so (Matt. 24:44-47; 1 Cor. 3:11-15; 9:24-25). This brings glory and honor to God and will bring praise in the end. It also demonstrates that there is real faith in the life of a believer, resulting in good works being done in the service of God (Eph. 2:10; Jas. 2:18).

Revelation 2:5 (Ephesus):

"Remember therefore from whence thou art fallen, and repent, and do the first works; or else I WILL COME UNTO THEE QUICKLY, and will remove thy candlestick out of his place, except thou repent."

Revelation 2:10 (Smyrna):

*"**Fear none of those things which thou shalt suffer:** behold the devil shall cast some of you into prison, that **YE MAY BE TRIED; and ye shall HAVE TRIBULATION ten days; be thou FAITHFUL UNTO DEATH,** and I will give thee a **crown of life."***

Revelation 2:16 (Pergamos):

*"Repent, or else **I will come unto thee quickly** [suddenly], and will **fight against them** with **the sword of my mouth."***

Revelation 19:15 says that at the visible Second Coming of Christ to earth, *a sharp sword* goes out of His mouth and He smites the nations with it on the day of God's wrath.

Revelation 2:22-23, 25 (Thyatira):

*"Behold, I will cast her into a bed, and them that commit adultery with her [Jezebel] **into GREAT TRIBULATION**, except they repent of their deeds.*

*And I will KILL HER CHILDREN with death, and all **the churches** shall know that I am he which searcheth the reins and hearts: and I will give unto every one of you according to your works . . . But that which ye have already **hold fast till I come."***

Revelation 3:2-3 (Sardis):

*"**Be WATCHFUL,** and strengthen the things that remain, that are ready to die: for I have not found thy works perfect before God. Remember therefore how thou hast received and heard, and HOLD FAST, and repent.*

*If therefore **THOU** [church age believers] **shalt not WATCH**, I will come on thee [quickly] **AS A THIEF**, and thou shalt not know what hour I will come upon thee."*

Once again, the same posttribulational "as a thief" warning to "watch" that Jesus and Paul gave to the churches is reiterated by John. There are many in the professing church of Jesus Christ who are not living for God. Some are unsaved hypocrites (Matt. 24:45-51; 25:11-12), while others are actually backslidden or lukewarm Christians who will suffer loss and be ashamed at the coming of Christ (1 Jn. 2:28).

Revelation 3:10-11 (Philadelphia):

*"Because thou hast **kept the word of my patience**, I also will **keep thee from** [ek: out of, out from within] **the hour of temptation** [not tribulation], which shall come upon all the world, **to TRY THEM** that dwell upon the earth. Behold, **I COME QUICKLY**, hold that fast which thou hast, that no man take thy **crown**."*

This church is the faithful church that will be given special grace during the "hour of temptation" that will "come upon the whole world. The whole world, at the time John wrote, probably refers to the Roman Empire (the only part of the world that really counted to the Romans), and the trial that was coming refers to the growing persecution and hostility against Christians under Domitian in the mid-90s, and various future emperors. Although Christians would not be removed from the earth, they would be kept through it, faithful to the end (read further comments for a futurist application of Revelation 3:10 on page 104).

[Note: The seven churches of Revelation are a picture of the spiritual condition of the churches that exist in the last days. They are not told they will be raptured before the things that John saw in the book of Revelation come to pass (i.e., the Great Tribulation). Rather, they are told to watch, hold fast, and be faithful unto death till the Lord comes.]

Revelation 6:12-17:

*"And I beheld when he had opened the sixth seal, and, lo, there was a great earthquake, and **the SUN BECAME BLACK AS SACKCLOTH of hair, and the MOON BECAME AS BLOOD; and the stars of heaven fell unto the earth** [Day of the Lord cosmic signs] . . . and the heaven departed as a scroll when it is rolled*

together; and every mountain and island were moved out of their places."

"And the kings of the earth, and the great men, and the rich men, and the chief captains, and the mighty men, and every bondman, and every freeman, hid themselves . . . in the rocks of the mountains;

*And said . . . Fall on us, and **hide us from the FACE OF HIM** that **sitteth on the <u>THRONE</u>** [the revealing of Christ at His Second Coming to earth], and from the [Day of the Lord] **wrath** of the Lamb; For the **great DAY of HIS WRATH is come**; and who shall be able to stand?"* (cf. Isa. 2:12, 17-19; Joel 2:1-3, 10-11; 30-31; Rev. 19:18-19).

It is obvious the sixth seal is the Day of the Lord, with all the accompanying cosmic signs, which occurs at the visible return of Christ, immediately after the Great Tribulation.

Revelation 7:9, 14-17:

*"After this I beheld . . . a great multitude, which no man could number . . . These are they which came out of **great tribulation** . . . Therefore are they before the **<u>THRONE OF GOD</u>**, and serve him day and night in his temple [shrine or dwelling place in heaven, Rev. 11:19]: and he that sitteth on the throne shall **<u>DWELL AMONG THEM</u>**.*

*They shall hunger no more, neither thirst any more; neither shall the sun light on them . . . For the Lamb which is **in the midst of the throne** shall feed them . . . **and God shall <u>WIPE AWAY ALL TEARS</u> from their eyes** [cp. Rev. 21:2-4]."*

John's vision "of a great multitude" in Revelation 7:9 takes place at the end of the Great Tribulation (7:13-14), not one thousand years later (compare a similar scene in Revelation 21:2-4).

Revelation 11:15, 18:

*"And the **seventh angel sounded**; and there were great voices in heaven, saying, **The kingdoms of the world are become the***

kingdoms of our Lord, *and of his Christ; and he shall* ***reign for ever and ever*** *. . . And the nations were angry, and thy [Day of the Lord]* ***WRATH IS COME***, *and* ***the time of the dead, that they should be JUDGED*** *[the post-trib resurrection of the saints on the last day], and that thou shouldest* ***give REWARD unto thy servants the prophets, and to the saints, and them that fear thy name . . .***" (cf. 2 Cor. 5:10).

Revelation 16:12, 15-16:

"*And the* ***sixth angel poured out his vial*** *upon the great river Euphrates; and the water thereof was dried up, that the way of the* ***kings of the east*** *[China and her cohorts?] might be prepared . . .*

"*Behold,* ***I come*** *AS A THIEF. Blessed is he that* ***WATCHETH***, *and keepeth his garments, lest he walk naked, and they see his shame. And he gathered them together into a place in the Hebrew tongue* ***ARMAGEDDON***.*"

Once again, Christ comes "as a thief" about the time of the battle of Armageddon, which comes at the end of the Tribulation.

Revelation 19:11, 14-15:

"*And I saw heaven opened, and behold a white horse; and he that sat upon him was called Faithful and True, and in righteousness* ***he doth judge and make war*** *. . .*

And out of his mouth goeth a sharp sword, that with it he should ***smite the nations***: *and he shall rule [or conquer] them with a rod of iron: and he treadeth the winepress of* ***the fierceness and wrath of Almighty God***. *And he hath on his vesture and on his thigh a name written, King of kings and Lord of lords.*"

Revelation 21:2-4:

"*And I John saw the holy city,* ***new Jerusalem***, *coming down from God out of heaven, prepared as a* ***bride*** *adorned for her husband.*

And I heard a great voice out of heaven saying, Behold, the **TABERNACLE** *[abode, the holy city]* **OF GOD** *is with men, and he will* **DWELL WITH THEM**, *and they shall be his people . . .* **And God shall** **WIPE AWAY ALL TEARS** *from their eyes [cp. Rev. 7:17]; and there shall be no more death, neither sorrow, nor crying . . . for the former things are passed away."*

The Question of the Rapture in Revelation 3:10-11

Revelation 3:10-11 states: *"Because thou hast* **KEPT THE WORD OF MY PATIENCE**, *I also will* **KEEP THEE FROM** *[Gr: ek, out of, out from]* **THE** **HOUR OF TEMPTATION**, *which shall come upon all the world, to* **try** *[Gr: peirazo: examine, scrutinize, prove] them that dwell upon the earth. Behold, I COME QUICKLY:* **HOLD FAST** *which thou hast, that no man take thy crown."*

Pre and midtribulationalists believe this passage of Scripture absolutely guarantees that Christians (i.e., the true and faithful believers), will be kept out of a period of time of great testing and trial (i.e., the Great Tribulation) which is going to come upon the whole world. They believe there is no way to reconcile posttribulationalism with this passage of Scripture. But Revelation 3:10-11 can easily be reconciled with the posttribulational Rapture view when considering the following:

First, the phrase, "kept the word of my patience," is a phrase implied in Revelation 13:10: *"He that leadeth into captivity shall go into captivity: he that killeth with the sword must be killed with the sword. Here is* **the patience** *and the* **faith of the saints**.*" During the time of the Great Tribulation, many Christians will be "taken into captivity" by the forces of the Antichrist, who is given power to make war and overcome the saints (Rev. 13:7). Anyone that refuses to worship the Beast or receive his mark will die by the sword (Rev. 6:9-11; 13:10, 15-16). This is when "the patience" and "the faith [trust in God and His Word in perilous times] of the saints" will matter the most.

There is also the *"**hour** [not seven years] **of temptation** [not tribulation]*," which could mean the general time of the Tribulation or it could be the literal hour that people will face when they are "tried" and have to decide whether they will deny Christ and take the mark of the Beast and live—or—not deny Christ and thus refuse the mark and die (Rev. 20:4). Thus, to insist that Revelation 3:10-11 guarantees that a pretribulational Rapture is going to happen, when it does not clearly say that, is presumptuous to say at the least. The promise to "keep thee from" could mean to be *kept completely out of* something (such as, the "hour of temptation") or it could mean that the saints will be *kept through it* or *kept from denying Christ* with the help of God during a short time of great temptation while facing execution. Just the fact that the Lord Jesus tells the seven churches to *"**hold fast** till I come"* (Rev. 2:15) and *"be faithful **unto death**"* (Rev. 2:10), implies faithful overcoming and a *spiritual preservation* out of it all, not a physical removal.

Jesus prayed for His disciples, saying—*"I pray **not that thou shouldest take them out of the world**, but that thou shouldest **keep them from** the evil [one]"* (Jn. 17:15). Our Lord prayed here to the Father on behalf of believers for their spiritual protection, and that they would be faithful and victorious through the trials and temptations that will test them while in the world. This can be applied to the meaning, "keep thee from," in Revelation 3:10. But let's assume that the promise to *"keep thee **from the hour** [not seven years] of temptation [not tribulation]"* actually does mean *physical* removal and not just spiritual preservation. That still does not *guarantee* or prove the Rapture happens *before* the Tribulation. Why? Because even though it may imply that, it still does not actually say that!

105

Second, there are areas of the world today that are known to be faithful to God's Word. For example, let's say many American Christians in the "Bible Belt" remain faithful to the Word of God. They might be spared some (not all) of the effects of the Tribulation because of their strength in numbers and God's divine protection and blessing. Just as when many Jews fled Nazi Germany in World War II to other countries, millions of fleeing Christians could find refuge in pockets of the world where the Antichrist will not be able to exercise control as easily as in other nations that are not faithful to the gospel of Jesus (such as in Europe, Asia, and the Middle East). That is why Christians everywhere need to be faithful to God's Word and keep taking in sound Bible doctrine often, evangelizing, making disciples, and being "salt" and "light" to their own nation, wherever that may be.

Another possibility is that the church is raptured posttribulationally, and then the Day of the Lord wrath is poured out upon a Christ-rejecting world. The fall of religious Babylon (led by the Pope?), at the end of the Tribulation, comes in one day and in one hour. Revelation 18:8a, 10b states: *"Therefore shall her plagues come in ONE DAY, death, and mourning, and famine; and she shall be utterly burned with fire . . . Alas, alas, that great city Babylon [Rome, Vatican City, or rebuilt Babylon?], that mighty city! For in ONE HOUR is thy judgment come."*

All true believers are commanded by God to *"COME OUT OF HER, my people, that ye be not be partakers of her sins, and that ye receive not of her plagues"* (Rev. 18:4)."

True believers will hear the voice of the shepherd and obey. This lines up with the warning messages to the churches of Pergamos (2:16), Thyatira (2:22-23), Sardis (Rev. 3:3), and the promise given to Philadelphia (Rev. 3:10). In short, the "hour of temptation" would deal primarily with unbelievers during the Great Tribulation and the Day of the Lord. Many will be converted to Christ as a result of that time of great distress and testing. It is God's final wake up call to humanity for their own good, when they are facing eternal damnation. Just as a cancer patient is given dangerous radiation treatment to destroy the deadly cancer cells and save his own life, so it will be during the Great Tribulation. God's intended purpose is for mankind to repent and be saved from imminent death and eternal damnation in hell (Zech. 13:8-9; 14:12, 16; Rev. 16:11; 20:11-15).

Tribulation vs. Wrath

We have seen how the Rapture and the Second Coming of Jesus Christ will come posttribulationally, "as a thief" in the night, immediately before the Day of the Lord wrath is poured out upon the world. Christians are commanded to watch and be ready for "that day," so it will not overtake them by surprise (1 Thess. 5:2-6). Now the question arises that if Christians must go through the Tribulation, won't they have to experience the wrath of an angry God as well? The answer is two-fold. First, divine wrath in the Bible is reserved for the enemies of God, not His people. God's "wrath" is coming upon all those who "believe not the gospel" and turn their backs on the truth, practice wickedness, and walk after their own lusts (Jn. 3:36; 2 Thess. 1:7-10; Heb. 4:2-3; Jude 4-5, 15-19).

Remember, God is sovereign and in control at all times. His divine judgments and wrath that comes upon people during the Great Tribulation will be directed at those who practice false religion and commit fornication (Rev. 2:14-16; 3:20-23), those who persecute and kill the saints (Rev. 6:10), those who follow after demons, practice idolatry, and do not repent of murder, witchcraft, sexual immorality, and theft (Rev. 9:20-21), those who worship the Antichrist and receive the mark of the Beast (Rev. 13:4-18), those who blaspheme the Name of God and refuse to repent of their wicked deeds (16:9, 11), those who join the false ecumenical (Babylon) religion of the last days (Rev.

18:2-8), and those who come to battle against Israel and the Lord in the end (Rev. 19:17-21).

The judgments will come in the form of seal, trumpet, and bowl judgments which include deadly plagues, famine, wars, and pestilence (Rev. 6), fire storms and possible nuclear bomb fall-out (Rev. 8:7-9; 16: 8-9; 17:16), demonic locusts released out of the bottomless pit that go forth upon the earth to harm *unsaved* mankind (Rev. 9:1-11), killer hail storms, a mighty earthquake (the largest ever), monster global tsunami tidal waves, wiping out every island and the coastlands (Rev. 16:18-21).

Secondly, though the awful judgments of God are *not directed at Christians*, many Christians who are living on earth during the Tribulation will experience at least some of its effects, such as hyper-inflation, hunger, and/or starvation due to food shortages (Rev. 6:6), possible nuclear fall-out and one third of the earth's water supply turning rancid (Rev. 8:7-11), wild beasts and huge invading armies killing off massive portions of the world's population (Rev. 6:4, 8; 9:14-16), and mass executions of those who refuse to worship the beast Antichrist and receive his satanic mark "666" (Rev. 13:15-18).

Jesus and Paul never promised that Christians would be exempt from all of the *effects* of the Great Tribulation. But they are exempt from the Day of the Lord wrath, which is a separate event from the Tribulation and comes immediately afterwards, when the cosmic signs in the heavens occur and the sixth seal of Revelation 6:12 is opened and the remaining Christians that are alive are then raptured.

Warning

Some of God's people will suffer chastisement (via plagues), or the sin unto physical death, if they partake of false ecumenical religious activity and fornication during the Tribulation period, and do not repent, cease their involvement, and come out of it (Rev. 2:20-24; 18:4).

Jesus said unless those days (the Great Tribulation) be shortened, there would be no one left alive to be saved, but for *the elect's sake* those days will be shortened (Matt. 24:22). Just as in any wartime situation, Christians are not exempt from being tortured, maimed, and/or brutally killed.

Concerning the future Antichrist, Revelation 13:7 states: *"And it was given unto him [the Antichrist] to **make WAR with the saints, AND TO <u>OVERCOME THEM</u>**: and power was given him over all kindreds, and tongues, and nations."*

Revelation 6:10-11 says the slain souls of the Tribulation martyrs in heaven will cry out, saying, *"How long, O Lord, holy and true, **dost thou not judge and avenge our blood** on them that dwell on the earth?*

*And white robes were given unto every one of them; and it was said unto them, that they should **rest yet for a little season**, **until THEIR FELLOW-SERVANTS** also and **THEIR BRETHREN, THAT SHOULD <u>BE KILLED</u> AS THEY WERE**, should be fulfilled."*

Modern dispensationalists say the martyrs in the Tribulation were not Christians before it got started, so they will miss the Rapture and have to go through it. They say the Trib saints are not the "bride of Christ" and Christ would NEVER permit His bride to go through the terrifying Tribulation, just prior to their wedding, marriage supper, and one thousand-year honeymoon. God, they say, doesn't want a bloody bride! That may suit "country club" Christianity in America, but it is not the way God has worked down through church history, neither in the majority of nations today!

Look at the long line of martyrs who were cruelly tortured, drowned, burned at the stake, skinned alive, beheaded, imprisoned, starved, impaled upon stakes, beaten to death, shot, hung, massacred, and raped at the hands of pagan Emperors, Catholic Inquisitors, Muslim jihadists, Nazis, Communists, and other enemies of the only true God (Yahweh) and His Son, Jesus Christ. Christians today are being persecuted, tortured, and killed all over the world for their faith, especially in Islamic lands (for more information, contact the *Voice of the Martyrs* at www.persecution.com).

Should we believe God would never let Christians today suffer at the hands of the Antichrist? Think again! Why would God be any different at the end of the age by not allowing Satan to "overcome" the Christian saints for a short season? The fact is, as we have seen in Revelation 6:10-11; 13:7, and been forewarned, God will allow Satan to overcome (kill) the Christian saints <u>ONE</u> <u>LAST</u> <u>TIME</u> during the coming Great Tribulation period.

Furthermore, just the fact that millions of people will become Christians during the Tribulation ought to slow down pre-trib dispensationalists from claiming that God will not allow Christians *today* to go through the future Tribulation. If God will allow them to go through it, why not us? Certainly He loves and cares for them too (and they will certainly need help from older Christians during that time). If some of the effects of the seal, trumpet, and bowl judgments listed in the book of Revelation were to fall upon the *Christians* in the Tribulation, then it could easily apply to the supposed exclusive "bride of Christ" as well.

The Concurrent View of Revelation

The visions of John are *overlapping* visions of judgment. The 6th seal (Rev. 6:12-17), the 7th trumpet (Rev. 11:15-18), and 7th vial (Rev. 16:15-19) judgments all converge at the end of the age, at the Second Coming of Christ to earth. Hence, they must be one and the same event (cp. Matt. 24:29-31; 42-44 and Rev. 16:14-16).

```
                                    Second Coming
Seals    1   2   3   4   5   6   7 (The great Day of God's wrath)
      Trumpets 1 2 3 4 5 6 7 (God's wrath is come)
             Vials 1 2 3 4 5 6 7 (The fierceness of God's wrath)
```

The Consecutive View of Revelation

The 7 seals (Rev. 5:1-5; 6:1-12; 8:1), the 7 trumpets (Rev. 8:2, 6-12; 9:1-21; 11:15), and the 7 bowls (Rev. 16:1-19) judgments all happen one after another, each set bringing on a new set of more intense judgments upon a Christ-rejecting world.

```
Seals  1  2  3  4 5 6 7
       Trumpets 1 2 3 4 5 6 7
                   Vials  1 2 3 4 5 6 7 (Second Coming)
```

Who is the Bride of Christ?

A major problem with traditional dispensationalism is that it fails to comprehend *who* the bride of Christ is and *when* the marriage of the Lamb takes place. The Bible teaches the bride of Christ is not an exclusive crowd of Christians! The bride, the Lamb's wife, is *both* the Old and New Testament saints, represented by the twelve tribes of Israel and the twelve apostles of the New Testament church (Eph. 5:25, 32; Rev. 21:9-14). Furthermore, the normal, literal, plain reading of scripture indicates that the marriage of the Lamb does not take place in heaven during the Tribulation, but rather, at the *posttribulational return* of Christ to earth.

Revelation 19:7, 9 says, *"Let us be glad and rejoice, and give honour to him: for **the marriage of the Lamb IS come** [not had come and went], and his wife hath made herself ready . . . And he saith* unto me, Write, Blessed are they which are **called unto the marriage supper of the Lamb**.*"*

Some pre-trib dispensationalists say that since only the New Testament Christians are the "bride of Christ," then Moses, King David, Solomon, John the Baptist and all the rest of the resurrected Old Testament saints and the Trib saints, at the Second Coming of Christ, are merely invited guests who are called to the marriage supper of the Lamb. But that *wrongly* divides the Word of Truth! There is only one resurrection at the end of the age for God's people, not two, and Israel is part of the redeemed bride of Christ (1 Cor. 15:23; 1 Thess. 4:13-17; Rev. 20:4-6; 21:9, 12)!

Remember also, the parable of the ten virgins teaches that the coming bridegroom (Jesus), and the wedding that takes place afterwards, is in the Matthew 24-25 context of the *posttribulational* return of Christ at the end of the age (Matt. 24:43-44; 25:13 cf. 22:2-14). Thus, the bride/wife of Christ = all God's people.

How to be an Overcomer

How will Christians patiently endure all things and be faithful even unto death during the horrible time of mass martyrdom during the Great Tribulation? They will overcome by knowing that God is in control, life and time is short, and the Lord Jesus will come again soon to avenge their blood.

*"**<u>Fear NOT</u> them which kill the body, but are not able to kill the soul**: but rather fear him which is able to destroy both soul and body in hell"* (Matt. 10:28).

*"For whosoever will **save** [cling to] **his life shall lose it**; but whosoever shall **lose** [sacrifice] **his life for my sake and the gospel's, the same shall save it**. For what shall it profit a man, if he shall gain the whole world, and lose his own soul?"* (Mk. 8:35-36).

*"And **TAKE HEED** to yourselves, lest at any time **your hearts** [mental attitude and focus] be overcharged [burdened, overtaken] with **surfeiting** [excessive eating and drinking, debauchery, pleasure seeking], and **drunkenness**, and **cares of this life** [material things, money, health, family, day-to-day living and the details of life, etc.], and so **that day** come upon you **unawares**. For as a snare shall it come on all them that dwell on the face of the whole earth.*

*__WATCH__ ye therefore, and __PRAY ALWAYS__, that ye may be counted **worthy to** [be wise and discerning to understand the times and] **escape** [Gr: ekpheugo: "to flee"] all these things that shall come to pass, and to stand before the Son of man"* (Lk. 21:34-36).

*"**Fear none of those things which thou shalt suffer**: behold, the devil shall cast some of you into prison, that ye may be tried, and **ye shall have tribulation** ten days [while enduring torture and awaiting execution?]: __BE THOU FAITHFUL UNTO DEATH__, and I will give thee a crown of life"* (Rev. 2:10).

*"But that which ye have already **hold fast till I come**. And he that **overcometh**, and **keepeth my works unto the end**, to him will I give power over the nations"* (Rev. 2:25-26).

God has rewards in store for those who remain faithful to Him to the end.

*"And **they overcame him** [Satan] by [their faith in] **the BLOOD OF THE LAMB**, and by __THE WORD__ of their testimony [unashamed, bold faith in God's plan for their lives], and they **LOVED NOT THEIR LIVES unto the death** [they were willing to die rather than deny Christ, thus obtain a more honorable resurrection]"* (Rev. 12:11 cf. Rom. 8:33-39; Heb. 11:35, 40).

*"Here is **the patience** [dying grace and peace of mind due to confidence and trust in God and His Word] **of the saints** [the suffering Christians in the Great Tribulation]: here are they that __KEEP THE COMMANDMENTS OF GOD__; and **THE FAITH** [sound Bible doctrine] of Jesus . . .*

*Blessed [happy] are the dead which **die in the Lord** from henceforth: Yea saith the Spirit, that they may **rest** from their labors"* (Rev. 14:12-13 cf. 13:7, 10; 2 Thess. 1:5-10).

*"Behold, **I come quickly**; and **my REWARD is with me**, to give to every man according as his work shall be . . . **Blessed are they that <u>DO</u> HIS COMMANDMENTS**, that they may have right to the tree of life, and may enter in through the gates into the city"* (Rev. 22:12, 14).

Conclusion

The Rapture and the Second Coming of Christ are two doctrines that are clearly taught in the Bible. Scripture reveals these two events will occur together, *on the same day*, immediately *after* the Great Tribulation, when Christ comes suddenly, "as a thief," to an unsuspecting, God-hating, Christ-rejecting world, just as in the days of Noah (Matt. 24:37). To say Jesus comes in the air at the Rapture, but not to the earth, and therefore conclude there must be two *separate* comings of Christ at the end of the age is ridiculous. If a plane flies over the earth, does that mean it is not part of the earth?

Furthermore, if Christ is going to take Christians back to heaven at the Rapture, why does He need to come into earth's atmosphere (with His reward) to gather us in the clouds and then take us back? Why not just catch us up right into the third heaven like Paul was (2 Cor. 12:2)? Also, to split hairs and say the *Day of Christ* is not the *Day of the Lord*, in order to come up with two separate comings of Jesus is just plain bad hermeneutics and wrongly divides the Word of truth! Christ is Lord!

It is a stretch of theology to say there are two phases of the single coming of Christ in a seven year period (pre-trib), or a three and one-half year period (mid-trib), or a twenty-one month period (pre-wrath).[2] Keep in mind, the two-phase Rapture teachings are theories.

One can teach them, but cannot dogmatically prove there are two separate phases that are several years or several months apart because the Scriptures do not clearly teach that anywhere! However, the single phase, post-trib coming of Christ, as a thief, with His mighty angels, in flaming fire, to gather together (rapture) the "elect" church (Matt. 24:29-31; 1 Thess. 4:16-17), and then descend with the armies of heaven to earth, in order to bring wrath and destruction (on the Day of the Lord) upon all those who persecuted the Christian church and attacked Israel during the Great Tribulation (Zech. 14:3, 12; Matt. 24; 1 Thess. 5:2-4, 9; 2 Thess. 1:7-10; Rev. 19:11-21), fits perfectly and harmoniously with all the prophetic teachings of the Old Testament prophets, Jesus, and the apostles.

Some pretribulationalists accuse their posttribulationalist brethren of being "used by Satan" to steal away the believer's hope in the "any moment" coming of Jesus to rapture believers. But it is not fair to make such a charge against posttribulationalists when, in fact, the scriptural and exegetical burden of proof remains in the pretribulationalist's court. The truth is, Jesus did give us signs to watch for and so did Paul!

When the man of sin (Antichrist) is revealed, *then* we can get excited about the fact that we are entering the Tribulation and our gathering together to be with the Lord Jesus in the air (via the Rapture) is near or at hand, and not before (Matt. 24:15, 29-31; 2 Thess. 2:1, 3). It is then (when Christ comes) that the simultaneous resurrection and judgment of the just and the unjust shall occur on the last day (Dan. 12:1, 2; Matt. 13:30, 49, 50; 25:31-46; John 5:28, 29; 6:39, 40, 44, 11:24; Acts 24:15; Rom. 2:5-16; 1 Cor. 15: 21-23; 2 Tim. 4:1; 2 Pet. 3:10; Jude 14-15; Rev. 11:15-18; 20:11-15).

Christians need to be *doctrinally, mentally, and spiritually prepared to face whatever may lie ahead*, even persecution and martyrdom at the hands of the coming Antichrist, as we wait and watch for the key signs that indicate our Lord's return is near. When

Jesus comes, He will raise the "dead in Christ" (Jn. 11:24; 1 Cor. 15:23; 1 Thess. 4:15-17), gather His elect (Matt. 24:31; 2 Thess. 2:1), take vengeance on the lost (Matt. 24:38-39; 2 Thess. 1:7-10; Rev. 19:11-21), judge and reward the believer's works (1 Cor. 3:11-15; 2 Cor. 5:10), and inaugurate the Age to Come (2 Tim. 4:1; Rev. 21:1).

Posttribulationalism consistently maintains normal, literal, and grammatical rules of interpretation. It can answer virtually anything thrown at it whereas, pre, mid, and pre-wrath cannot. The other three plainly violate, more or less, the rules of biblical interpretation, and are novel and of recent origin, hence, in my opinion, should be abandoned.

[2] The pre-wrath Rapture view has some merit because it sees the Rapture and the Day of the Lord as happening immediately *after* the Tribulation, when the cosmic signs in the heavens appear (Joel 2:30-31; Matt. 24:29). The main difference between the pre-wrath and post-trib view is the *length* of the Day of the Lord, several months vs. one day, respectively. After the Rapture, it really won't matter how long the Day of the Lord lasts for believers.

How Shall We Live in Light of the Future Rapture?

This book is written in the year 2000. If the post-trib Rapture view is correct—and I believe it is—then it will take *at least* until 2007 (2000 + 7 years), or later, before the Rapture will happen. Why? Because none of the key signs that indicate the return of Christ is imminent have taken place yet (e.g., a rebuilt Jewish Temple in Jerusalem, the Antichrist, the Great Tribulation, and the Armageddon campaign). In the meantime, Christians should continue to work, pay the bills, raise their families, evangelize, make disciples, and *watch for the biblical signs* that tell us Christ is about to return. Don't sell your home and head for the hills, or spend a lot of time and money on books that say Christ may come back at "any moment."

2013 Update

This book is now being reprinted in the year 2013. This means, according to the post-trib view, the Rapture cannot occur until *at least* 2020 (2013 + 7 years), or later, since a seven-year peace treaty has not been signed yet between the coming Antichrist ruler (someone from the revived Roman Empire) and "many nations" (including Israel), which will introduce the final 70th Week of Daniel that will last seven years before the Second Coming of Christ (Dan. 9:24-27 cp. 7:21-27).

By me saying the above, **I am in no way predicting the day, or hour, or even the year of Christ's return!** It is a simple deduction to add Daniel's 70th Week of seven years to our present 2013 date. In the meantime, as stated previously above, Christians should continue to live their lives normally and watch for the key biblical signs that warn us Christ's return is near.

[Note: Even though many political leaders are currently calling for a "New World Order," under a "one world" (global) socialist government (led by the UN), and many false religious leaders are seeking to unite all world religions in spiritual "oneness" and peaceful co-existence, and apostasy from the truth and gross immorality are rampant, this still does not mean the end is upon us. Not until the Antichrist comes on the world scene, *and begins to rule over the nations*, can we then assume the end is near. His reign of terror will last 42 months before Jesus Christ returns (read Revelation 13 and 19).]

6

Answers to Commonly Asked Questions

Question #1
Won't we know the exact day of the Second Coming of Christ if the Rapture is posttribulational?

Jesus said no man knows the day and hour of His return (Matt. 24:36). However, we will be able to know it is near when the "abomination of desolation" (i.e., the setting up of an image to be worshipped) is committed by the Antichrist in the rebuilt Jewish temple in Jerusalem, which will begin the brief period of time known as the Great Tribulation (Matt. 24:15, 21; 2 Thess. 2:4). Only then can a person start counting down the days to the Second Coming of Christ.

However, God reserves the right to "cut short" the length of the Great Tribulation (Matt. 24:22) for the sake of the elect, and so, we cannot be absolutely certain it will last for the entire time of 1,260 days or 42 months (Rev. 11:3; 13:5). But even if it does go the entire time, that still does not contradict Jesus' words in Matthew 24:36. When Jesus spoke of His Second Coming, no one knew the day or hour (not even Him), just as no one knows today (so beware of anyone who claims they have figured out when Jesus is going to return). Obviously the people in the time of the Great Tribulation will be able to countdown the days to the return of Christ. But it won't be until the Antichrist *reveals* himself in the Temple in Jerusalem that we can actually set a date (assuming Christ returns on day 1,261).

Keep in mind, Christ will not come back until the cosmological "day of the Lord" signs (i.e., the sun and moon shall be darkened, stars falling from the heavens, etc.) occur, immediately *after* the Great Tribulation (Joel 2:30-31; Matt. 24:29).

Question #2

What is the point of the Rapture if Christians go up to meet the Lord in the air, only to then come right back down at the Second Coming of Christ?

The purpose of the Rapture is three-fold. First, Christians are not appointed for the Day of the Lord wrath, which is total destruction via fire purging of all Christ-rejecting sinners on earth (2 Thess. 1:7-10), along with a cleansing of the earth (2 Pet. 3:10).

Second, mortal flesh and blood cannot inherit the kingdom of God; thus, one needs to be glorified to enter into the kingdom on the new earth (1 Cor. 15:50). At the Rapture, all the living and dead saints will be raised up and transformed in a moment, in a twinkling of an eye.

Third, Jesus is coming back in glory with all His saints who will escort Him back to earth as a conquering king (Zech. 14:5; Rev. 19:14).

[Note: Our meeting with Christ in the air is likened to a welcoming party that leaves a house in order to go down the road to meet an honored guest, visiting dignitary, or triumphant military leader and escort him back home or to town.]

Question #3
What about 2 Thessalonians 2:6-8? Will
the Holy Spirit be removed in the Tribulation?

In 2 Thessalonians 2:1-3, Paul addresses the matter of the coming of the Lord and our gathering together to be with Him at the Rapture, which is preceded by the revealing of the "man of sin" (the Antichrist). He then states in verses 6 and 7:

> *"And now ye know **what withholdeth** that he might be revealed in his time. For the mystery of iniquity doth already work: only he who now letteth will let, until **he be TAKEN OUT** [Gr: ek] **OF THE WAY**. And then that WICKED [the Antichrist] be revealed . . .".*

Pretribulationalists say the Restrainer (the Holy Spirit), which *indwells every believer* in the dispensation of the Church Age, is keeping the Antichrist from coming on the scene right now. When the Rapture occurs, the Holy Spirit will also be removed from the earth because the Christians will be snatched off the earth and taken back to heaven. Is this sound Bible doctrine? What saith the Scriptures?

2 Thessalonians 2:7-8 does not say the omnipresent Holy Spirit will be removed from the world during the 70th Week of Daniel. Rather, it probably refers to the fact that the *restraining influence* of the Holy Spirit will be removed. Then the world, which loves its sin and hates the truth (2:10-12), can have exactly what it wants— complete independence from God. But it will be under the tyrannical control of Satan (Rev. 13).

It is like two boxers wanting to fight, but a referee is standing in between them, keeping them back from exchanging punches. But when the referee steps back and stops restraining, the fighters can go at it again. The referee does not have to *leave the earth* to stop restraining; rather, he simply steps out of the way. In the same way, the Holy Spirit will let the Antichrist come with the power of Satan to deceive a lost and rebellious world with a lie (2 Thess. 2:9-12).

Many pre-trib Rapture teachers say Christians must first be removed from the planet because if they are still here they will expose the Antichrist, and then he won't be able to deceive the world. But that is nonsense! The truth is, hundreds-of-millions of people will adore the Antichrist and give him homage when he appears. He will be their darling leader and messiah. They couldn't care less about what some born again, "fundamentalist" Christians in America (or anywhere) have to say about him! Remember, the Antichrist, along with the false prophet (maybe a pope or Muslim leader), will be working mainly in spiritually dead Europe, secular Israel and the Islamic Middle East. True Christianity is not well-liked in those parts of the world.

The communists in Russia and China won't care (at least not at first). Neither will the Hindus, Buddhists, Jainists, Zoroastrians, Spiritists in the Far East, or the New Agers in the West. The Muslims and most Jews won't have a clue. The New World Order globalists, secret societies (e.g., the Masonic Lodge), atheists, deists, agnostics, secular humanists, socialists, astrologers, pagans, witches, and rock 'n' roll crowd won't care at all (or turn from their ways). Neither will the most of the vile and perverse homosexuals (sodomites), lesbians, feminists, abortionists, and drug/porn dealers and addicts.

Big labor unions (which endorse and support every liberal politician out there) will back the Antichrist. Colleges and universities will laud him. The liberal media will praise and extol him. Many crooked politicians, radical (leftist-leaning) judges, and lost lawyers (ACLU-types) will join his "politically correct" agenda to advance their godless goals. Many "big players" in the corporate world, media, and the military will support his evil schemes. Liberal clergymen (blind guides leading the blind) will publicly endorse him in their pulpits and in print.

He will be voted the "Man of the Year" and top the latest poll charts. Billions of people from all walks of life will sell out their own souls and blindly follow the Antichrist, like hogs to the slaughter. All the unsaved people of the nations will idolize him. The UN will fully endorse him. Armies will follow and protect him and do his evil bidding. Apostate religious leaders and entire denominations will think the false prophet and the Antichrist are wonderful and that they were "sent by God" to bring about global peace and unity. The apostate World Council of Churches (made up of Orthodox, Protestants, Anglicans, etc.) and the Vatican will have no problem with him and will back him completely. Keep in mind, most liberal and traditional denominations today do not believe in a literal coming Antichrist. Many doubt or scoff at the idea there is even a real devil! Many do not even know what the true gospel is and don't even care!

Meanwhile, Christians oftentimes cannot even get bad politicians out of office or get bills passed in Congress to end unrighteousness in the nation (e.g., abortion). Many Christians don't vote and many more rarely, if ever, share the gospel with others, much less make disciples. Add to that the sorry fact that many popular, but undiscerning and gullible, evangelical, emergent, and charismatic leaders (who think that *anyone* who says they believe in Jesus or God is a Christian or child of God) will probably partake in ecumenical "dialogue" with the false prophet and the Antichrist when they first appear.

No! Christians do not have to be removed from the earth in order for Satan to have his way with an evil world that is already completely devoted to false religion, sinful pleasures, and idolatry. If the Antichrist appeared on television/radio today and announced that he was the devil's man, the world would still run to him, as long as he offered them what they want. And he will, at the price of their own souls.

Question #4

Is the "falling away first," mentioned in 2 Thessalonians 2:3, referring to Christians being raptured or is it referring to a worldwide defection from God and Christianity?

Some believe the "falling away" (Gr: *apostasia*: "departure") refers to Christians departing (or being raptured) off the earth by Christ *before* the "man of sin" (the Antichrist) appears (cp. 2:7-8). Others believe it refers to the great falling away or departure *from the faith* that Paul warned would come in the latter days (see 1 Tim. 4:1; 2 Tim. 3:1-5), which results in multitudes believing "a lie" and following the Antichrist (2 Thess. 2:10-12).

It seems to me, according to the context, it refers to the great falling away from the faith. Why? Because in verses 1 and 2, Paul writes about "our gathering together unto him (Christ)," which clearly speaks of the Rapture. He then says in verse 3, "that day shall not come except there be a falling away first." (Note: *that day shall not come* is in italics in the King James Bible, which means it was added by the translators, thus is not in the original Greek manuscripts). It would be redundant to say our gathering together to be with Christ via the Rapture cannot happen until the Rapture first occurs.

Furthermore, in verse 2, Paul downplays the notion that the Day of Christ (i.e., the coming of the Lord to gather together believers) is "at hand" (near, imminent), since the key signs of verse 3 had not yet come to pass. In short, to view a falling away in verse 3 as referring to the Rapture (the departure of the saints to meet the Lord in the air) seems to strain the normal reading of the text.

Finally, even if one holds to the translation in verse 2 as saying, "the Day of the Lord *has come* [is present]" (NAS), that still does not affirm the pretribulation Rapture view. Why? Because, as we have seen previously in this book, the Day of the Lord comes immediately *after* the Tribulation (Matt. 24:29-31). (See appendix chart: Daniel's 70th Week). But even if the Day of the Lord did include the 70th Week of Daniel or the Tribulation (which it doesn't), it would still not affirm a pre-trib Rapture.

I believe the Thessalonians, who were experiencing persecution and tribulation (1:4), thought they might have entered into "the" Great Tribulation (thus knew it meant that it would only get worse in the world before Christ comes to gather them together at the end). So of course they were "shaken in mind" or troubled, as many would be today if they believed they entered into the time of the Great Tribulation. But Paul assured them that they were *not* in that time of trouble, and Christ's return was *not* near (or at hand or even had come) because the Antichrist was *not* on the scene yet, and any letter or message stating otherwise was bogus.

Keep in mind, the Thessalonian Christians were going with their understanding of Paul's first didactic (clear systematic instruction) letter written to them about the sudden Rapture *immediately before* the Day of the Lord wrath occurs (1 Thess. 4:13-5:6), which agreed with our Lord's clear prophetic teachings in Matthew 24 that taught a post-trib return of Christ. Paul simply reminded them of what he previously taught, that before the Rapture and Day of the Lord/ Christ occurs, the Antichrist would have to come and sit in the temple of God in Jerusalem (2 Thess. 2:3-5 cp. Matt. 24:15). All this clearly eliminates the "any moment and signless" pre-trib Rapture position.

[Note: To claim the Second Coming of Christ was "in prophecy" (previously revealed) and the Rapture was "a mystery" (previously undisclosed), thus,

125

cannot occur at the same time is a faulty assumption. The "mystery" of the Rapture dealt not so much with its timing, per se (although it is linked with the post-trib Day of the Lord); but rather, *how and in what order* the living and the dead are going to be resurrected or raised up and changed at the Lord's return, *at the sounding of the last trump*, when the kingdom of God and the fiery Day of the Lord wrath comes at the end of the Tribulation (**1 Cor. 15:51-52**; 1 Thess. 4:13-17 cf. 2 Thess. 1:7-10; **Rev. 11:15, 18**; 16:15-19). Also, to claim everybody in the Tribulation will know Christ will return soon, thus will be ready for it, is also an assumption. The truth is, most unbelievers refuse to hear or believe (and even scoff at) anything the Bible says (including future events), thus will be caught unawares and overtaken "as a thief in the night" (1 Thess. 5:2-5). This will be the case during the Great Tribulation, especially with the strong satanic delusion brought on by the Antichrist (2 Thess. 2:8-12). Christians, on the other hand, are told to watch and be ready for the return of Christ (1 Thess. 5:6).]

Question #5
Is the Church raptured in Revelation 4:1, 2?

Pretribulationalism places the Rapture of the Church at Revelation 4:1-2 which says:

> *"After this I looked, and, behold, a door was opened in heaven; and the first voice which I heard was as it were of a trumpet talking with me; which said, **COME UP HITHER**, and I will show thee things which must be hereafter. And immediately I was in the spirit: and, behold, a throne was set in heaven, and one sat on the throne."*

In the context of John 4:1-2, John is told to come up and that is all. There is no actual mention of millions of other Christians going up to heaven at that time. To teach this is when the Rapture occurs is an assumption, not based on any solid biblical evidence from the text. One should not build their rapture theology on Revelation 4:1-2, especially when Revelation 16:15-16 says Christ is coming as a thief at the time of Armageddon, at the end of the Tribulation (1 Thess. 5:1-2).

Question #6
Is the Church not mentioned in Revelation 4-18?

Pretribulationalists say the Church is raptured in Revelation 4:1-2 and there is no mention of the Church again until the Lord Jesus comes back in Revelation 19. Is that true? What saith the Scriptures?

Revelation 14:13 states: *"Blessed are the dead which **die in the Lord** from henceforth: Yea, saith the Spirit, that they may rest from their labors; and their works do follow them."*

If one is "in Christ" then they are "in the Lord," who is the Head of the Church. Many pre-tribbers insist that the Holy Spirit will be removed from the planet at the Rapture. Thus, they say new Christian converts, who become born again during the Tribulation, are "in the Lord," but not "in Christ," since the Holy Spirit supposedly will not be there to baptize them into the body of Christ! But that is ridiculous, if not heretical! Christ is Lord!

Is Christ divided? Of course not! (1 Cor. 1:13). Can one become born again without the Spirit? Impossible! (Jn. 3:3, 6; Rom. 8:9). The Holy Spirit is omnipresent and He is not going away during the Tribulation. He will stop restraining Satan, but He is not leaving the planet. Furthermore, if one dies *in the Lord*, they die *in Christ*. That means that they (the Tribulation saints) are also part of the Church, the body of Christ.

Also, why would the Spirit of God give the seven churches all that instruction and exhortation to hold fast and be faithful unto death, even saying clearly that some of the faithful would be *put into tribulation* (Rev. 2:10), if the Church is absolutely not going to be there? Why would Jesus show John the things that are to take place in the future, after He spoke of the spiritual condition of the seven churches in Revelation 2-3, if there is absolutely no connection with the rest of the book? And what does it mean to the churches to be an "overcomer" in Revelation 2-3 if the Rapture happens before the Tribulation, unless, to be an overcomer really means one is willing to die for the faith during the Great Tribulation, or any other time (Heb. 11:35-40)?

The truth is, the Christian church is mentioned in chapters 4-18!

- They are THE SAINTS AND THE MARTYRS THAT DIED "IN THE LORD" during the Great Tribulation.
- They are identified as those that came out of the Tribulation and "washed their robes in the blood of the Lamb" (Rev. 7:14).
- They are "the brethren" that are accused by Satan and overcame him by the blood of the Lamb (12:11-12).
- They are "the saints" that the Antichrist is given power to make war with and overcome, and are told to be patient (13:7-10).
- They are those that "die *in the Lord* from now on" (14:12-13).
- They are "my people" that are commanded by God to "come out" of the one-world, ecumenical (united), Babylon system of false religion (Rev. 18:4).

That is the whole point of the book of Revelation. Jesus will come back *once*, right after the Great Tribulation, to reveal Himself to the whole world and deliver/gather the elect of God, just as Jesus, Paul, and John all taught in the New Testament (Matt. 24:22, 29-30; 1 Thess. 5:1-5; 2 Thess. 1:7-10; Rev. 16:15-16; 19:11-21). So is the Church mentioned in chapters 4 through 18? You be the judge.

Question #7

If present-day Christians might end up going through the Tribulation, does this mean they should prepare for it now?

Although it is always wise to be prepared for disasters that might happen by having a few extra months food supply, alternative energy sources, better home security, etc., at this point, I wouldn't do it based on the not yet impending Tribulation. Since the Antichrist is not in power yet, we simply are NOT in that time. Furthermore, if the first 3 ½ years of Daniel's 70ᵗʰ Week is a time of relative peace and prosperity, as most prophecy teachers say (unlike the second half of Daniel's Week of 42 months of great tribulation), then, in my opinion, it is not crucial to prepare until the 7-year peace treaty is made between the Antichrist and many nations (Dan. 9:27; Rev. 13:5). Why? Because that would give people 3 ½ years to prepare for the hard times that will definitely come afterwards. This could save people time, money, and possibly their testimony by those around them, by not going overboard or starting way too early (especially since it may take several more years, or even decades, to transpire yet).

Keep in mind, the apostles Paul, Peter, and John never mentioned making physical preparations (such as storing up food) for the future, but they did stress that we should always be spiritually sober, awake, and holy (1 Thess. 5:6; 1 Pet. 1:15-16; Rev. 2:22). This does not mean we shouldn't do any sort of preparing at all (God wants us to be wise by thinking ahead), but the main thing is to *remain faithful to Christ*, even unto death (martyrdom), no matter what happens (Rev. 14:12-13).

Christians should NEVER become obsessive or anxious, but instead, trust in God at all times. The result will be peace of mind, not fear (see Job 13:15; Phil. 4:6-9). How? By knowing that our all-powerful, righteous God not only knows everything and is in control at all times, but also cares and will let things go only so far. This means Christians need not panic or become distraught when we see things falling apart all around us, but rather, have confidence in our loving heavenly Father who knows our needs, and has a plan that is being worked out to His glory, even in the midst of terrible trials and suffering, and for our deliverance and exaltation in the end.

[Note: Joseph's divinely inspired dream prepared Egypt for 7 years of extreme drought by first having seven years of plenty (Gen. 41:15-36). In a similar way, if the church today is still here on earth during Daniel's 70th Week, those who recognize the signs of the times will have 3 ½ years to prepare for the final 42 months of great tribulation. Even then, it may not matter much, depending on where one is located and what happens when all hell literally breaks loose on earth, and economic collapse, disasters, and crime explodes. But it does not hurt to consider one's options and begin taking some precautions in view of our worsening times, and before the actual Tribulation arrives (read Proverbs 27:12).

There are many websites that provide information about making and storing your own food, shelf-life, tools and gear, etc. Make a list of what you think you'd need. This does NOT mean Christians should be like some extreme "preppers," who build bomb shelters, do self-defense drills every weekend they can, and seem bent on shooting anyone who might trespass on their property if and when society collapses, causing total panic and chaos. Although I am a strong supporter of the 2nd Amendment of the United States, and the right to bear arms and defend ourselves, even from a biblical standpoint (Ps. 144:1; Lk. 22:36), our lives should be spent seeking and doing the Lord's will, and living in peace with all men, as much as possible.

One last very important thing—**always be ready to share the gospel with others**. It is the words of eternal life and billions of people need to hear it. For help in becoming an effective soul-winner, read my book, *Evangelism and Christian Apologetics (Crash Course Training in One-on-One Evangelism).*]

Question #8
I attend a church that staunchly teaches a pre-trib Rapture. What should I do?

First of all, don't cause a big fuss or run away. As with most disagreements, communication is the key. I would go to your pastor and humbly tell him what you have been learning, and even offer a copy of this book. Tell him your concerns about some interpretation problems that modern Acts 2 dispensationalism has and consider a more accurate interpretation. Remember though, the pre-trib Rapture is a big issue for many evangelicals, especially fundamentalists. They have been hammered with it for many decades now, and usually won't be easily convinced. It will take time (one discussion won't do it) and solid arguments (which is one reason I wrote this book), even if they are willing to listen to you or discuss it.

Furthermore, know that if you are in any sort of leadership position (such as a teacher), if you do not hold to an imminent, pre-trib Rapture belief, it may cost you your ministry there. Many evangelical, and especially fundamentalist churches today also require belief in an imminent, pre-trib Rapture to be a member. Some even make it a matter of orthodoxy, though belief in the *timing* of the Rapture is not an essential of the faith. And there are not a whole lot of good churches I know of in the United States that even teach a post-trib Rapture, since so much of evangelicalism today has been inculcated with Acts 2 (pre-trib) dispensationalism.

I have found that most members in these churches do not really understand dispensationalism at all (and many have not even heard the word before, so be ready to define it). Not only that, most students in seminary and pastors have not been seriously taught anything but classic Acts 2 dispensationalism. It will be an uphill battle to see any changes in these churches, but the truth must be told. Even if they do not adopt a post-trib position, discussing it will at least result in more awareness, and possibly prepare them in case the Tribulation comes in their lifetime.

[For further help in understanding dispensationalism, read my book, *Acts One Dispensationalism*. This concise book examines Acts 2, Progressive, and Mid-Acts views, and offers a more biblical solution.]

Question #9
Who is the Antichrist and the False Prophet?

There is much speculation about who the Antichrist might be, and his evil cohort, the false prophet. From a biblical futurist perspective, they are both diabolical leaders (one political and one religious) who will arise in the last days, shortly before Christ's return. Together they will deceive the entire world (except the elect of God) by the power of Satan, via lying signs and wonders (2 Thess. 2:9).

No one knows for sure who these two literal men are yet, but it will become obvious when they take power and begin to do their satanic agenda, as revealed in the Bible. Some key prophecies that identify the Antichrist (a.k.a., the Beast, the son of perdition, the man of sin) are:

- He will arise out of the revived Roman Empire (Europe), as the final ruler of the "ten-toe" or "ten-horn" confederacy of nations (Dan. 2:41-43; 7:23-24; 9:26), and gain authority over the entire world for 42 months (Rev. 13:5, 7).
- He will receive a deadly head wound, but will be healed, and cause the world to marvel (Rev. 13:3, 12).
- He will create temporary economic prosperity and world peace, through his unparalleled oratorical, intellectual, commercial, political, and military genius (Dan. 7:23-25; 8:23-25; Rev. 13:4).

- He will make a 7-year treaty with Israel, but break it 3 ½ years later (Dan. 9:27).
- He will sit in the temple of God (a rebuilt Jewish temple in Jerusalem) and arrogantly declare himself to be God (Matt. 24:15; 2 Thess. 2:3-4).
- He will mercilessly persecute the saints (Christians) and put many to death, plus anyone else who will not worship his image (Dan. 7:21; Rev. 13:7, 10, 15).
- He will implement a cashless society that requires his mandatory identification mark (666) in person's right hand or forehead (computer chip?), in order to buy or sell anything, or else be killed (Rev. 13:16-18).

The false prophet (maybe a demon-possessed pope?) will also exercise authority, perform satanic miracles, and cause people to follow and worship the Antichrist as their messiah (Rev. 13:11-14). Together, they will lead the world to the brink of total destruction at Armageddon, but will be defeated and thrown alive into the lake of fire when Jesus Christ returns (Rev. 19:11-20).

(For more information, read two informative books, *Unmasking the Antichrist* by Ron Rhodes and *Global Peace and the Rise of the Antichrist* by Dave Hunt.)

Question #10
What about Preterism, which says Matthew 24 and the book of Revelation has already been fulfilled?

Full preterism (Latin: *praeter*, meaning "past") is a teaching that says *all* the prophecies Jesus gave in Matthew 24 and most of Revelation, were fulfilled in the first century. They get this from Jesus' statement in Matthew 24:34: *"Verily I say unto you, **this generation** shall not* *pass, till **all** these things be fulfilled."* This differs from the more commonly held teaching that says Matthew 24 was only *partially* fulfilled in the first century and some prophecies remain yet to be fulfilled, such as the *personal and physical* Second Coming of Christ at the end of the age (24:30). What is the answer to this division? What saith the Scriptures?

Matthew 24 indeed speaks to the first generation of believers who would *see the destruction of the Jerusalem temple* in AD 70, because not one stone was left upon another after the Roman army decimated Jerusalem, just as Jesus foretold (24:2). However, the Olivet Discourse not only predicts the destruction of the Jewish temple, but also the literal Second Coming of Christ, immediately *after* the tribulation. If Jesus only meant the generation of Jews in the first century, then Matthew 24 is a false prophecy because Christ obviously did not return in the clouds, with His mighty angels and all the saints, in the first century to rescue Israel.

At this point, full preterists can only spiritualize away the literal text to mean that Christ's "coming" refers to His *spiritual* presence in *the judgment of Israel* by the Romans in AD 70. But that contradicts the many Bible prophecies concerning the physical coming (presence) of the Messiah to Jerusalem, when His feet literally touch down on the Mount of Olives and He then goes forth to defend Jerusalem and destroy *the heathen nations* (not Israel) at the end of the age (cp. Joel 3:15-16; Zech. 14:2-4; Acts 1:11; 2 Thess. 1:7-10; 2:8; Rev. 19:11-21). Since scripture interprets scripture, we must compare the Olivet Discourse in Matthew 24 with a similar passage recorded in Luke to solve this matter and bring unity, since there can only be one true meaning.

Luke 21:24 gives a key detail not recorded in Matthew 24:

*"And they [the Jews] shall fall by the edge of the sword [by the invading Roman army in 70 AD], and **SHALL BE <u>LED</u>***

AWAY CAPTIVE INTO ALL NATIONS: and Jerusalem
shall be trodden down of the Gentiles, UNTIL THE TIMES
OF THE GENTILES be fulfilled."

History proves that since Jesus spoke those words, "the times of the Gentiles" has been going on for almost two thousand years. After the Romans ruled Israel (and before that the Babylonians and Greeks), then came the Byzantines, the Arab Muslims, Catholic Crusaders, more Muslims, the Ottoman Turks, and the British. Then the Jews began returning home in large numbers after World War II, with the rebirth of national Israel in 1948. Even though the State of Israel is sovereign over Jerusalem today, it is still being *trodden down by Gentiles* (partly by the Muslims) and will be during the final 42 months of Great Tribulation.

Jesus said AFTER the times of the Gentiles are fulfilled, the DAY OF THE LORD COSMIC SIGNS (the sun turns dark, the moon turns blood red in color, the stars from heaven fall, etc.) will *then* occur, just before the literal, visible, and bodily SECOND COMING of Jesus Christ in power and great glory (Matt. 24:29-31; Luke 21:25 cf. Joel 2:30-31; 3:14-15). Thus, full preterism is a *false* teaching and should be rejected by all students of Bible prophecy. All the signs of the fig tree must take place in order for the Olivet Discourse to be completely fulfilled. This had to include **the worldwide dispersion of the Jews** in the first century and the land of Israel being left desolate for *a long time* (Luke 21:24).

Partial preterism (which sees Matthew 24 as being partially fulfilled in AD 70) and dispensational futurism (which sees most of Matthew 24 as being still in the future) affirm the parable of the talents in Matthew 25:14-30, where Jesus (the Lord of the parable) taught about His going away for a LONG TIME (25:19) and then returning to settle accounts with His servants (Israel) at the end of the age. "This generation" must refer to the generation that sees all the signs of the fig tree come to pass, which can only refer to the generation that is alive sometime *after* the Jews return from worldwide dispersion back into the land of Israel (Luke 21:24). They will experience the final hard labor pains, or great tribulation that lasts 42 months before the end (24:14), while Jerusalem is still trodden down by the Gentiles (Matt. 24:21; Rev. 11:2).

The Great Tribulation will begin with the "abomination of desolation" (referring to the Antichrist) taking place in the holy place, in Jerusalem (Matt. 24:15 cp. 2 Thess. 2:3-4). Preterists believe this refers to the sacrilege committed by the Romans in 70 AD, when they desecrated the Jewish Temple in Jerusalem by entering into it with an image of Caesar. Though that may partly apply, this near-far prophecy is related specifically to *the* Day of the Lord, when the cosmic signs in the heavens occur *immediately after* the Tribulation, just prior to the visible and physical return of Jesus Christ at the end of the age (Luke 21:25-27).

Others have suggested that the meaning of "this generation" (Gr: *genea*) may refer to men of the same stock, family, or race— the Jews. In other words, even though Satan and his minions have tried to exterminate the Jews down through the centuries, they have miraculously survived as a distinct people group and returned to their homeland. God has preserved the Jews (even though most have remained in unbelief till now) and they will indeed see *all these things come to pass*, and a remnant will turn to the Lord and be saved in the end (Rom. 11:25-29), no matter what (see *Believer's Bible Commentary* by William MacDonald).

Regardless of which view is correct, in my opinion, considering all the things that have happened since 1948, it appears that our present generation could very well be "the" generation that will see the literal Second Coming of Christ to earth.

[Note: Preterism denies the prophecies that pertain to the Jewish people and nation of Israel in the last days and replaces them with the Church (this is a heresy called, Replacement Theology), and is held by the Catholic Church and certain Protestants that hold to Covenant Theology and amillennialism or postmillennialism, such as Presbyterian and Reformed churches. For more information, Google *Preterism* and read my book, *Signs of the Second Coming of Jesus Christ and the End of the World*.]

A Final Word

In the end, the most important thing for every human being is not the *timing* of the Rapture, but rather, will they be *ready* to meet Christ when He returns? The Lord Jesus will judge the living and the dead at His appearing (2 Tim. 4:1; Rev. 11:15-18). He came from heaven the first time, in order to shed His blood and die on a cross to pay for your sins, then rose bodily from the dead (1 Cor. 15:3-4) so you can be saved from the penalty of sin—eternal separation from God in the lake of fire (Mk. 9:43; Rev. 14:9-11; 20:11-15).

Why did He do it? Because He loves you and wants to forgive you of all your sins (no matter how bad) and fellowship with you, forever.

John 3:16: *"For God so loved the world, that he gave his only begotten Son, that whosoever <u>believeth</u> in him should not perish [die and go to hell], but have everlasting life."*

What must you do to be saved?

Acts 3:19: *"Repent ye therefore, and be converted [to Jesus Christ], that your sins may be blotted out."*

Acts 16:31: *"Believe on the Lord Jesus Christ and thou shalt be saved . . ."*

Romans 10:9: *"That if thou shalt confess with thy mouth the Lord Jesus, and shalt <u>believe</u> in thine heart that God hath raised him from the dead, thou shalt be saved."*

Romans 10:13: *"For whosoever shall call upon the name of the Lord shall be saved."*

The choice is yours. God will not force you to believe in Christ, but He invites you to do so now. All who repent (change their mind and turn to God) and place their trust in His only begotten Son will be saved from the wrath to come. If you have not done so yet, simply confess to God right now that you are a guilty sinner, in need of Jesus Christ, the only Savior of sinners. Then, by faith, call upon the Lord to save you, based on what *He did for you* on the Cross. When you do, God says you will be forgiven and given the free gift of eternal life. That is God's promise to you and He cannot lie.

Then read the New Testament (start with the Gospel of John and Romans) and follow and serve the Master for the rest of your life.

[For help in getting grounded in Christianity, read two of the author's books: *The Fundamentals of the Christian Faith* and *Christian Discipleship and the Local Church.*]

Appendix I

Summary of Five Doctrines

1.   Doctrine of the Day of the Lord

1. The Day of the Lord is a phrase that appears 19 times in the Old Testament (Obad. 15; Joel 1:15; 2:1, 11, 31; 3:14; Amos 5:18, 20; Isa. 2:12; 13:6, 9; Zeph. 1:7, 14; Ezek. 13:5; 30:3; Zech. 14:1; Mal. 4:5) and 4 times in the New Testament (Acts 2:20; 1 Thess. 5:2; 2 Thess. 2:2; 2 Pet. 3:10), to express the time of God's extreme wrath. It is the "day of doom," "day of vengeance," and the "Great Day of God Almighty."

2. The Day of the Lord can refer to near *historical* judgment (Ezek.13:5; 30:3) or far (yet future) divine judgment (Zech. 14:1; 2 Thess. 2:2); thus it has occurred in the past (OT times) and will again in the future, at the Second Coming of Christ at the end of the age.

3. The Day of the Lord in the Old Testament came upon Israel as divine chastisement for her continual disobedience, idolatry, and unrepentant rebellion against the Lord their God (Isa. 1:2-7; 13:6-9).

4. The future Day of the Lord is a "unique day" of calamity, terror, and devastating judgment against God's enemies who follow Satan and come against Israel at Armageddon (Joel 3:13-16; Zech. 14:1-9).

5. The Day of the Lord will be preceded by cosmic signs in the heavens with thunders, lightning, great hail, stars (meteorites) falling from heaven, the sun being turned into darkness and the moon into blood (dark red color), and global seismological disasters (a great earthquake and worldwide tsunamis)—Joel 3:14-16; Matt. 24:29; Rev. 16:18-21.

6. The future Day of the Lord will be that day when the Lord Jesus Christ returns visibly to earth, in power and great glory, with His mighty angels, to judge and make war, right *after* the Great Tribulation at the end of the age (Matt. 24:29; 2 Thess. 1:7-10; Rev. 19:11-21).

7. The future Day of the Lord will happen suddenly "as a thief in the night" to an *unsuspecting* world, but not for believers who are told to watch and expect the Lord's coming (1 Thess. 5:2-5).

8. The future Day of the Lord will last one solar day (Zech. 14:7).

9. The future Day of the Lord (Day of Christ) will result in the deliverance of remaining Christians and a third part of Israel from their enemies (Zech. 12:9; 13:8; 14:12; 2 Thess. 1:7-10; 2:1-2).

10. The future Day of the Lord will result in the conversion of a remnant (1/3) of Jews in the land of Israel to Christ (Joel 2:28-32; Zech. 12:10; 13:8-9; 14:1-12).

11. The Day of the Lord will bring the passing away of our present earth, and a new heavens and new earth results (2 Pet. 3:10-12).

2.   Doctrine of the Second Coming of Jesus Christ

1. The Coming of Christ is His visible (not invisible, secretive, or as a spirit), bodily, and glorious return to Jerusalem, in Israel, at the end of the age (Zech. 14:4; Matt. 24:3, 27; Acts 1:9-11; Tit. 2:13; Rev. 1:7; 19:11-16).

2. The Coming of Christ will occur right <u>after</u> the Great Tribulation, when the cosmic signs in the heavens occur (Matt. 24:29-31).

3. The Second Coming of Christ is the day of the Lord (1 Thess. 4:14-17; 5:1-2) when **every eye** shall see Him (Matt. 24:27, 30; Rev. 1:7).

4. The Second Coming of Christ will result in the destruction of the Antichrist, the false prophet, and all the rest of unsaved humanity (2 Thess. 1:7-10; 2:8; Rev. 19:11-21).

5. The Second Coming of Christ will result in the resurrection of the dead, the final harvest, Judgment Day, and the eternal Kingdom of God (Matt. 13:39-42; 25:31-46; Jn. 5:27-29; 6:40; 1 Cor. 15:20-24; 51-53).

3.   Doctrine of the Rapture

1. The Rapture is the catching up or gathering together into the clouds, to meet the Lord in the air, of all who have died *in Christ*, and all those who are alive and *in Christ* at His coming (1 Thess. 4:15-17). It is the resurrection of all believers at "the last day" (Jn. 6:39-40), thus one generation (i.e., the last generation) of living Christians, *and only Christians*, will not experience physical death.

2. The Rapture will be instantaneous, in the twinkling (an estimated 1/40th of a second) of an eye (1 Cor. 15:52).

3. The Rapture will occur in tandem with the Day of the Lord, when the Lord Jesus comes *as a thief in the night* immediately *after* the Great Tribulation (Matt. 24:29-31; 1 Thess. 4:15-18; 5:1-4; Rev. 16:15-16). Believers are told to watch and be sober and spiritually awake and ready for "that day" (1 Thess. 5:4-6).

4. The Rapture will be a single event (not several partial raptures), since it happens at the single coming (parousia) of the Lord at the end of the age (Matt. 24:3, 30; 1 Cor. 15:23; 1 Thess. 4:17).

5. The Rapture will transform the believer's mortal/corruptible body into an immortal/glorified body (1 Cor. 15:50-54) and will bring all believers together to be with the Lord forever (1 Thess. 4:17).

4.   Doctrine of the Last Trump (or Seventh Trumpet)

1. The Last Trump in 1 Corinthians 15:52 is synonymous with the 7th (and last) Trumpet Judgment in Revelation 11:15.
2. The 7th (Last) Trump will sound by an archangel, and be accompanied with a shout from the Lord Jesus Himself, as He descends from heaven (Matt. 24:31; 1 Cor. 15:52; 1 Thess. 4:16).
3. The 7th (Last) Trump will commence with the resurrection of the dead and the Rapture of all the elect (living saints) into the clouds to meet the Lord in the air (Matt. 24:31; 1 Cor. 15:52; 1 Thess. 4:16-17).
4. The 7th (Last) Trump will result in the kingdoms of this world becoming the kingdoms of our Lord at the visible Second Coming of Christ to earth, immediately after of the Tribulation when the day of the Lord's wrath is come, and God destroys His enemies (Matt. 24:29-31; Rev. 11:15, 18).
5. The 7th Trump will commence with Judgment Day for the dead and the Bema (Judgment) Seat of Christ to reward all the saints and them that fear God (Rev. 11:18 cp. Matt. 13:38-43; 24:31; 1 Cor. 15:23-24; 2 Cor. 5:10), followed by the celebration of the marriage supper of the Lamb (Rev. 19:7-9).
6. The 7th Trump inaugurates the reign of the Lord Jesus Christ over the kingdoms of the world for ever and ever (Rev. 11:15).

5.   Doctrine of Persecution and Martyrdom of Believers

1. Down through history, God's people have not been immune to suffering, slander, persecution, and/or martyrdom.
2. Jesus warned that if the world hated Him, it will also hate His servants (Matt. 10:22, 24-25, 34-36 cp. Lk. 6:22; Jn. 15:18-20; 16:2).

3. Jesus said not to fear those who can kill the body, but fear him (God) who can destroy body and soul in hell (Matt. 10:28).

4. God commands *all believers,* experiencing trials and persecution, to be *patient* and *remain faithful,* **even unto death** (Rev. 2:10).

5. God knows the hardships and sorrows of His children and will reward those who suffered for the sake of Jesus Christ (Matt. 19:29; 2 Tim. 4:6-8; Heb. 11:26, 35-40; Rev. 2:13; 14:12-13).

6. Christians are not exempt from tribulation in general, nor the future Great Tribulation in particular (Jn. 16:33; 1 Thess. 3:3-4; Rev. 2:10; 6:9-11; 7:13-14; 13:5, 7, 15), but they are excluded from God's wrath that will happen on the Day of the Lord, immediately after the Tribulation (Matt. 24:29-31; Rev. 11:15; 14:17-19; 16:14-16).

7. In order to overcome and persevere in adversity, believers are commanded by God to always walk by faith and trust God no matter what (**Job 13:15**), be wise and aware of Satan's schemes (Eph. 6:11-13), ready in mind to endure suffering (Rom. 8:17-22), and rejoice and pray always in everything (Eph. 6:18; Phil 4:6-9).

8. God uses suffering and the fires of persecution to refine (purify, sanctify) His people as gold and to bring Him glory (Job 23:10; 1 Pet. 5:10-11; Rev. 6:10).

9. If martyrdom becomes inevitable, God promises to be with us always and give grace and strength to face it (Matt. 28:20; 2 Tim. 4:17-18).

10. In the end, God will wipe away every tear from the eyes of His people, and there will be no more sorrow, pain, or death (Rev. 21:4).

Appendix II

Questions for Acts 2 Dispensationalists to Ponder

1. Are the Old Testament saints are "in Christ"?
2. If the Old Testament saints are not in Christ, or have no connection with the Church, the body of Christ, how do you then explain Romans 11:15-24, which says the Gentiles (wild branches) were grafted into the "good olive tree" (the holy root being Christ), along with the natural branches (Israel)? Also, if the OT saints are not "in Christ," how are they raised to eternal life when only those who are in Christ shall be made alive at the end (1 Cor. 15:21-22)?
3. When does the "last day" (Jn. 6:40) occur?
4. The "dead in Christ" are raised *first* at the Rapture (1 Thess. 4:16). If the OT saints are in Christ, and they are raised on "the last day," along with all who believe in Christ (Jn. 6:39-40), how can you hold to a pre-trib Rapture, since the Christians who are alive at Christ's coming will *not precede* the resurrection of *all* those who died in Christ and/or all who believe in Christ on the last day?
5. When does the Day of the Lord happen and does it involve the Rapture?

6. If the Day of the Lord is the day that Christ comes as "a thief in the night" at the Resurrection (Jn. 6:40; 1 Cor. 15:20-24 ; 1 Thess. 4:16; 5:2, 4), and is preceded by the cosmic signs in the heavens (Joel 2:30-31; 3:14-15; Matt. 24:29; 2 Pet. 3:10), which happens immediately *after* the Great Tribulation at the visible Second Coming of Christ during the battle of Armageddon (Joel 3:16; Matt. 24:30; Rev. 16:14-15), how then can you teach that the Rapture-Resurrection is a *signless* event and/or "imminent" (near, can happen at any moment)? (cf. 2 Thess. 2:1-3).

7. If the Matthew 28 Great Commission applies to the church today, and goes to the end of the age (at the Second Coming of Christ), then how can the church be removed before then?

8. If the pre-trib Rapture was never really taught by anyone in church history until John Darby came along in the 1800's (and later, C.I. Scofield, Ryrie, and others), should you put so much stock in it? Have you considered other Rapture views, such as classic post-trib (Moo, Gundry) or historic (post-trib) premillennialism (Ladd)?

Daniel's 70th Week, the Great Tribulation, and the Day of the Lord

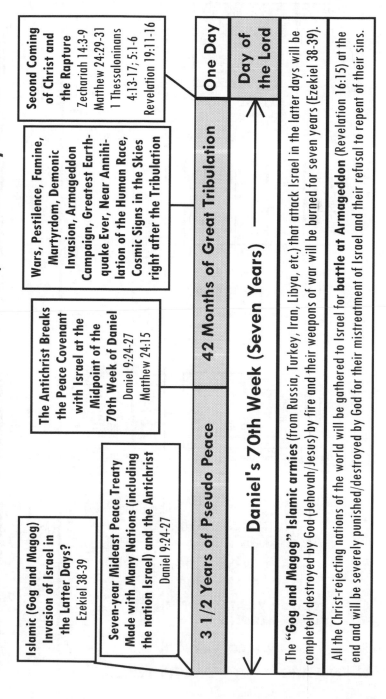

Islamic (Gog and Magog) Invasion of Israel in the Latter Days?
Ezekiel 38-39

Seven-year Mideast Peace Treaty Made with Many Nations (including the nation Israel and the Antichrist
Daniel 9:24-27

The Antichrist Breaks the Peace Covenant with Israel at the Midpoint of the 70th Week of Daniel
Daniel 9:24-27
Matthew 24:15

Wars, Pestilence, Famine, Martyrdom, Demonic Invasion, Armageddon Campaign, Greatest Earthquake Ever, Near Annihilation of the Human Race, Cosmic Signs in the Skies right after the Tribulation

Second Coming of Christ and the Rapture
Zechariah 14:3-9
Matthew 24:29-31
1 Thessalonians 4:13-17; 5:1-6
Revelation 19:11-16

One Day

Day of the Lord

3 1/2 Years of Pseudo Peace | **42 Months of Great Tribulation**

— **Daniel's 70th Week (Seven Years)** —

The **"Gog and Magog"** Islamic armies (from Russia, Turkey, Iran, Libya, etc.) that attack Israel in the latter days will be completely destroyed by God (Jehovah/Jesus) by fire and their weapons of war will be burned for seven years (Ezekiel 38-39).

All the Christ-rejecting nations of the world will be gathered to Israel for **battle at Armageddon** (Revelation 16:15) at the end and will be severely punished/destroyed by God for their mistreatment of Israel and their refusal to repent of their sins.

147

A Dispensational Overview of Four Ages

Gentile

- Adam and Eve
- Noah and 3 Sons
  Shem, Ham, Japheth
  (Genesis 1-11)

Jew / Israel

- Abraham
- Isaac and Jacob
- 12 Sons of Israel
- Egyptian Bondage

- Moses, Aaron, and Levite Priests
  Bloody Animal Sacrifices

Christian Church

- Mystery Form of the Kingdom of God (Matthew 13:11-43)
- Dispensation of the Grace of God in Christ (Ephesians 3:2-6)

Kingdom

- The Age to Come
  New Heavens and New Earth

Genesis 1-2 (ca. 4100 B.C.) **CREATION**

Genesis 3 (Fall of Man) **CORRUPTION**

Genesis 6-7 **CATASTROPHE**
Noah and the Great Flood (ca. 2450 B.C.)

Genesis 11:1-9 **CONFUSION**
Tower of Babel (ca. 2325 B.C.)

Genesis 12:1-9 **CALLING**
Abraham (ca. 2090 B.C.)

Moses and Israel's Exodus From Bondage in Egypt (ca.1445 B.C.)

The Law Required Circumcision, Washings (Baptisms), Sabbath-Day Keeping, Feast Days, Animal Sacrifices

John 19:30
Matthew 27:51
Colossians 1:20; 2:14

CROSS
JESUS **CHRIST**
(4 B.C.—29 A.D.)

The 12 Apostles

Paul's Apostleship (ca. 32—67 A.D.)

Only One True Gospel
- Acts 10:39-45; 1 Cor. 15:3-4
- Peter, Apostle to the Jews
- Paul, Apostle to the Gentiles
- Galatians 2:7-9

CONSUMMATION
SECOND **COMING**
of CHRIST

Christ Shall Reign Forever and Ever
Daniel 2:44; 7:13-14, 18
Revelation 11:15

THE JEWISH OLIVE TREE (Romans 11:1-26) Gentiles Grafted in as Wild Branches

THE WHOLE FAMILY OF GOD (Ephesians 2:19; 3:6, 15) Fellowcitizens of Heaven

THE BRIDE OF CHRIST, THE LAMB'S WIFE (Revelation 21:9-14) All OT and NT Saints

Recommended Reading and Ministries for Further Study of the Rapture and Dispensational Theology

(To order, contact Christian Book Distributors at 1-800-CHRISTIAN or Google *Dispensationalism*.)

Steve Urick, *Acts One Dispensationalism* (Why the Church Existed in Acts 1 and the Answer to the Acts 2:38 Water Baptism Controversy). Available at Amazon.com

Tim Lahaye, *The Rapture*, Multnomah Publishers (Defends the pre-trib Rapture view.)

Dave Hunt, *Global Peace and the Rise of the Antichrist*, Harvest House (go to *www.thebereancall.org*)

Renald E. Showers, *There Really is a Difference*, The Friends of Israel Gospel Ministry (Compares Covenant and Dispensational Theology.)

Charles Ryrie, *Dispensationalism Today*, Moody Press
Basic Theology, Moody Press

Archer, Feinberg, Moo, *The Rapture: Pre, Mid, or Posttribulational?* (Zondervan Publishing)

Marv Rosenthal, *The Pre-Wrath Rapture of the Church*, Thomas Nelson Publishers

Robert Gundry, *The Church and the Tribulation*, Zondervan Publishing (Defends the post-trib Rapture.)

George Eldon Ladd, *A Theology of the New Testament*, Eerdmans Publishing (Defends the post-trib Rapture and historic premillennialism.) A must-read one volume work.

Craig L. Blomberg, *A Case for Historic Premillennialism (An Alternative to "Left Behind" Eschatology)*, Baker Academics (A must-read book that includes many quotes by the early church fathers.)

Louis Berkhoff, *Systematic Theology*, Eerdmans Publishing Company (Defends post-trib Rapture and amillennialism.)

Dwight Pentecost, *Things to Come*, Zondervan Publishing

Henry C. Theissen, *Lectures in Systematic Theology*, Eerdmans Publishing Company

Dr. John Walvoord, *The Rapture Question*, Zondervan Publishing

Craig A. Blaising and Darrell L. Block, *Progressive Dispensationalism*, Baker Academics

Paul Enns, *The Moody Handbook of Theology*, Moody Press (Compares all the major theological views.)

Believer's Bible Commentary by William MacDonald, Thomas Nelson Publishers (An outstanding one-volume commentary.)

Charles Baker, *A Dispensational Theology*, Grace Bible College Publications (Defends mid-Acts 13 Dispensationalism and is available through the *Berean Bible Society*. See ministry list below.)

Cornelius R. Stam, *Our Great Commission* (Defends Acts 9 Dispensationalism, printed by the *Berean Bible Society*. See ministry list below.)

Ministries

The Berean Call with Dave Hunt and T.A. McMahon (One of the best apologetic ministries in America). Contact them at 1-800-937-6638 or *www.thebereancall.org* or write to: The Berean Call, P.O. Box 7019, Bend, OR 97708. Ask for their very informative free monthly newsletter.

Middletown Bible Church is an online ministry that has many helpful articles on dispensationalism, apologetics, and other theological issues. Go to *www.middletownbiblechurch.org*.

Fundamental Evangelistic Association is a dispensational, gospel and apologetics ministry that offers tracts and booklets that exposes liberalism and apostasy in our world today. They also offer an outstanding monthly magazine called, *Foundation (A Magazine of Biblical Fundamentalism)*. Go to *www.feasite.org* or write: FEA, 1476 W. Herndon Ave., Suite 104, Fresno, CA 93711, U.S.A. Ask for a free sample pack.

Berean Bible Society offers the free monthly magazine, *The Berean Searchlight,* that promotes mid-Acts Dispensationalism. The BBS says the church did not exist until Paul got saved in Acts 9 and water baptism is *not* to be practiced during our present age. To learn more, go to *www.bereanbiblesociety.org* or write to: N112 W17761 Mequon Rd, Germantown, WI, 53022-0756 or call 262-255-4750.

[Charles Baker's book, *A Dispensational Theology,* is available through the BBS ministry, along with all the writings of Cornelius Stam. Their writings have also been called ultra-dispensationalism.].